THE OPEN
Royal St George's 2003

Hazleton Publishing Ltd
5th Floor, Mermaid House, 2 Puddle Dock, London EC4V 3DS
Hazleton Publishing Ltd is a member of Profile Media Group Plc

Published 2003 by Hazleton Publishing Ltd

Copyright © 2003 The Championship Committee Merchandising Limited

Statistics of 132nd Open Championship produced on a
Unisys Computer System

Excerpt from *Decisions on the Rules of Golf* on page 63
© The Royal and Ancient Golf Club of St Andrews

Assistance with records provided by Peter Lewis, Stewart McDougall and Salvatore Johnson

Photographs on pages 8-19 courtesy of Stephen Szurlej
Photographs on pages 27, 31, 51 (top right), 57 (bottom left), 60, 62 (left),
66, 80 (right), and 83 courtesy of Getty Images
Photograph on pages 98-99 courtesy of Helen Hudson

A CIP catalogue record for this book is available
from the British Library

ISBN: 1-903135-28-1

Type and layout by Davis Design
Printed in Great Britain

Sandwich Bay

WRITERS

Robert Sommers

Michael Aitken

Andy Farrell

John Hopkins

Lewine Mair

Michael McDonnell

PHOTOGRAPHERS

Michael Cohen

Phil Inglis

EDITOR

Bev Norwood

Authorised by the Championship Committee of The Royal and Ancient Golf Club of St Andrews

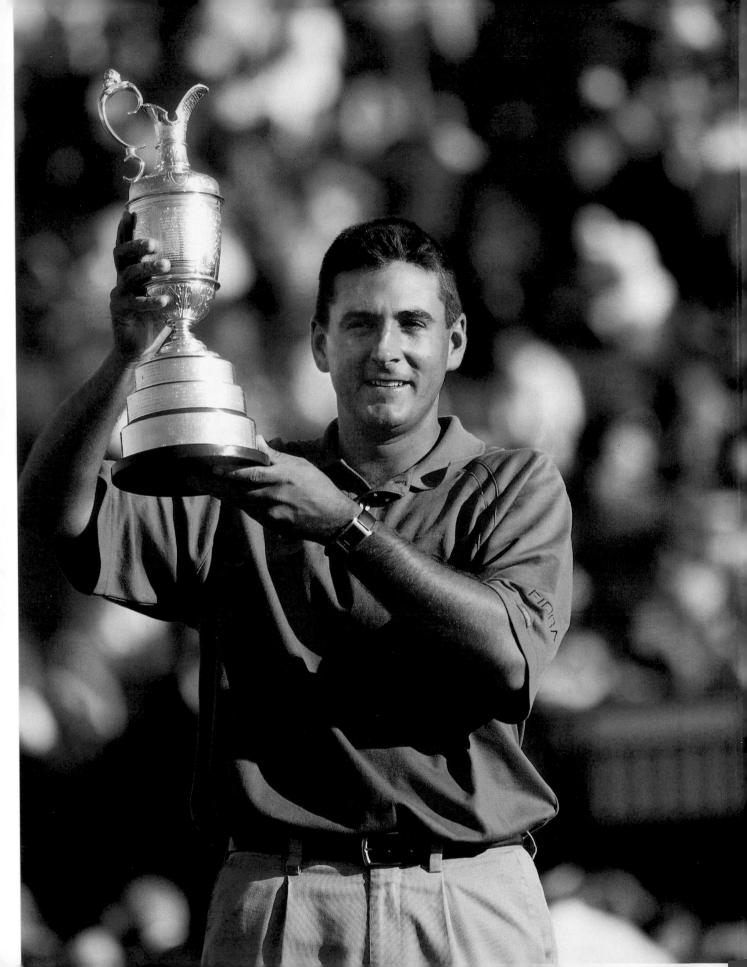

Foreword

By Ben Curtis

I remember being at the presentation, and hearing the words "champion golfer of the year" followed by my name, and it was unbelievable. I cannot describe how I felt right then. I had been in a zone, focused on what I was doing, and I didn't really think about winning until afterwards.

I wish my family could have been with me but fortunately, I had my fiancée, Candace Beatty. We had a great time that week. As I said then, I'm from Kent, Ohio, and to be in Kent, England, all of the people there made me feel right at home. The fans were great.

This was my first time to the Open Championship. I came in just trying to make the cut and compete on the weekend. I did that, and then I played probably the best weekend of my life. I had won in the past, but not at this level. I was concentrating on what I had to do and let my work speak for itself. If that had not been good enough, fine, I could have lived with it.

I've always felt my game was good for major championship golf, because you don't have to be 20 under par. You can shoot right around par and have a chance to win. And I feel that's where my game is the best.

There are so many professional golfers who just dream of winning a major championship, and I did it on my first try. I got a lot of lucky bounces, but some that didn't go so well, too. I know the names on the trophy, and that I am in great company. I may have felt before that I didn't belong, but I know now that I do.

Ben Curtis

The Venue

A New Challenge

By Michael McDonnell

That eminent essayist Bernard Darwin came to the reluctant conclusion almost a century ago that even the most idyllic golfing terrain has to change constantly to present a relevant challenge to the developing playing skills of each generation.

He had in mind a favourite landscape in the southeast corner of England over which the links of Royal St George's stretch and where skylarks, linnets, and kestrels adorn the scene on the edge of the English Channel but which, for all its natural beauty, was at the time being criticised for certain weaknesses in golfing design.

Some of the leading golfers of the day, Freddie Tait and Edward Blackwell among them, dismissed it as a "one shot" course in which the player hit over a sand hill, then ran up to see what had happened on the other side. In consequence Darwin felt obliged to pick up his pen in 1910 and write, "Why do they want to change this adorable place?" But he added, "I know they are perfectly right and I have even agreed with them."

The irony is that if Darwin were to cast a celestial eye over the links as prepared for the 2003 championship, he would have noticed compelling evidence that the doctrine of change as the price of survival still holds true. How else to explain the sighting of nine new tee positions that extended the course by 246 yards from its playing length for the 1993 championship?

The crucial point about such changes that had been fashioned by architects Donald Steel and John Salvesen is that they still placed heavy emphasis on strategic play and had not been designed solely to test muscle power.

Moreover, the underlying strength of this area of rugged Kent coastline is that it has the scope and capacity to absorb such amendments while retaining the essential character that has challenged the great heroes of the game ever since its golfing potential was recognised in 1887 by the original designer, Dr Laidlaw Purves, a redoubtable Scottish surgeon domiciled in London. With his fellow countryman Henry Lamb, Purves had

On the par-5 seventh hole, left is the preferred side of the fairway. The sixth hole (preceding spread), even in a bowl, is protected by wind.

A tee shot at the fourth hole takes on a towering bunker.

been searching for territory in southern England that was akin to the links of their homeland.

Curiously enough, according to Horace Hutchinson in 1899, the subsequent popularity and prominence of Royal St George's stemmed from its relative proximity to London. He called it "a London club with its green at the seaside," and he was in no doubt that its rapid elevation as an important venue with an Open Championship only seven years after opening its doors (won by a 23-year-old Hampshire professional John Henry Taylor) had as much to do with its influential membership as its "special excellencies as a golf green."

It was the first venue outside Scotland to host an Open Championship when Taylor won in 1894, and the subsequent succession of victors since that time reflects not only the quality of its enduring challenge but the strength of the great figures of each era who equalled its demands. Indeed, it is this ability of truly imaginative players to fashion their skills to whatever circumstances they may encounter from squalls, gales, crosswinds, uneven lies, capricious bounces, and uncontrollable fairways that sets them apart from their rivals.

None more so than Arnold Palmer in winning the 1975 PGA Championship at Sandwich and summoning such ingenuity and technique to fashion an eagle 3 from the awesome Canal Hole (the 14th, then 508 yards). He played downwind by drilling a three-iron approach that never rose more than eight feet from the ground to finish within six feet of the

The 10th hole has a long, narrow green that is raised and drops away on all sides towards bunkers.

flagstick for a single putt. Arnie was pleased with his effort and explained later, "I just turned the three iron in a little."

Indeed, it is a mark of this broad canvas that Royal St George's presents to both amateur and professional that so many key events have been held upon its links. The 1904 Amateur Championship held particular significance when Walter Travis became the first American citizen to defeat the home players, though much credit for the success of the modest but straight hitter was given to his centre-shafted putter which caused a stir a first sight and was subsequently banned by the authorities until a much later date.

His triumph ruffled a few feathers including those of Horace Hutchinson, one of his victims, who wrote, "However good a player Mr Travis might be (I have not the slightest hesitation in classing him as a very fine player), it implies a measure of good fortune that he should win the championship the first time of asking."

In essence Travis had "found a way" to play the course—a game plan in modern parlance—that was strictly observed and by which the player never overstretched himself but simply charted a safe route that took the

Features of the 14th hole include a narrow fairway and a prevailing wind blowing against the golfer.

hazards out of play. Deane Beman observed a similar strategy in winning the 1959 Amateur title at Royal St George's, although his Walker Cup teammate Jack Nicklaus took first honours by winning the 36-hole St George's Challenge Cup before the championship.

When Walter Hagen arrived for the 1928 championship, he had just suffered a humiliating 18-and-17 defeat at the hands of Archie Compston in a challenge match at Moor Park and consequently went into strict personal training, even to the point of "locking up my little black book" and refusing to accept "the tempting phone calls." Such monkish self-discipline by the renowned bon vivant certainly paid off, because he went on to win his second title at Sandwich.

Hagen's first victory in 1922 held more drama. The press were so certain he was about to score a runaway victory that some published the fact before his round was completed and newspapers were being sold on the course announcing the new champion. However, Hagen and the press were obliged to endure a anxious wait as George Duncan came to the last hole needing a 4 to tie, but he missed the green left into a dip that has since become known by some as Duncan's Hollow and took three to get down.

Duncan's Hollow figured prominently in Sandy Lyle's historic win in 1985, although not with such disastrous effect. The young Scot could afford the cost of a fluffed chip from that same area, as the ball rolled back to his feet, and still take five strokes for victory to become the first home player since Tony Jacklin to win the Open.

The meteoric but brief career of Texan Bill Rogers reached its peak at Sandwich with his 1981 victory, and while debates may continue about the reason for his brief span, the abiding fact remains that for those four days he was the best in the world. Moreover, in

Round Royal St George's

No 1 442 Yards Par 4
A tee shot towards the left side of the fairway, although risky, offers an easier and shorter approach over three cross bunkers at the front of the green, which itself slopes away towards the back.

No 2 418 Yards Par 4
An additional 40 yards demands a big carry from the tee over the bunkers at the corner of this right-to-left dogleg, and even then, leaves a testing approach over a ridge which drops sharply down towards the green.

No 3 210 Yards Par 3
There are no bunkers, but the tee shot must be threaded towards a long narrow green, which sits back into the sand hills covered with thick rough, making the prospect of a precision chip shot for the ball missing the target extremely difficult.

No 4 497 Yards Par 5
The tee shot which takes on the towering bunker dominating this hole leaves a more manageable approach from the right-hand side of the fairway to a green that slopes from back to front with out of bounds immediately behind.

No 5 420 Yards Par 4
A judicious iron from the tee will find the plateau in the fairway and offer a view between the sand hills of the green but, with no mounds or bunkers to provide definition, the approach can be difficult to judge.

No 6 172 Yards Par 3
The Maiden, named after the high dune to the left of the green, is invariably protected by a capricious wind, and even though it sits in a bowl, makes club selection difficult—particularly in trying to avoid the perimeter of bunkers.

No 7 532 Yards Par 5
The preferred line for the tee shot favours the left side of the fairway to avoid running through into heavy rough on the right, but any shot that finds the fairway earns the chance of a birdie, provided the approach is not over-hit and runs through.

No 8 455 Yards Par 4
The new tee 39 yards farther back brings two new right-hand bunkers into play. So the tee shot must favour the left to set up what is still a demanding approach to a long and narrow two-tiered green.

No 9 388 Yards Par 4
The main problem for the tee shot is the crosswind, and positional play with an iron is the wiser strategy to find the right-hand side of the fairway and thereby minimise the prospect of the approach running off the sharp slope to the right of the green.

No 10 Par 4 414 yards
The long, narrow green is raised and drops away on all sides towards bunkers, thus making the precise position of the shot an imperative, particularly as an approach that is fractionally under-hit will roll back down the slope.

No 11 242 Yards Par 3
There is a more difficult angle of attack to the long green surrounded by five bunkers, because the tee has been moved back 26 yards and positioned farther right, while the putting surface requires serious study because of its subtle breaks.

No 12 381 Yards Par 4
The tee shot over a ridge must avoid a cluster of three bunkers well within damaging range. So the favoured alternative is to find a position in the fairway short of the trouble, and rely on short game dexterity for a birdie chance.

No 13 459 Yards Par 4
There is a new tee position to the right, but a new bunker on the left in the landing area means the tee shot is now menaced by sand on both sides, although the green with its central spine running front to back opens up for a second shot from the right.

No 14 550 Yards Par 5
A new green, sited close to the right-hand out-of-bounds fence which flanks the fairway from the tee, adds more menace. A narrow fairway, a stream (the Suez Canal) at 330 yards, and a prevailing wind blowing against and from the left make it the ultimate test.

No 15 475 Yards Par 4
The tee has been pushed to the right and a fifth bunker added to the driving area. But the real challenge is the approach, which must carry the three bunkers that extend to the front edge of the long green, which falls away to both left and right.

No 16 163 Yards Par 3
The green is virtually surrounded by deep bunkers and rises towards the back, but the swirling wind creates a more subtle problem to club selection and judgement. There were two holes-in-one here in the 1981 Open, one with a nine iron and the other with a five iron.

No 17 428 Yards Par 4
Even a good drive can leave the ball in an uneven lie among the humps and hollows, thus adding more difficulty to the approach to a raised green which is extremely shallow and likely to punish the slightest hint of hesitancy.

No 18 460 Yards Par 4
The tee shot played to the left allows the approach to take the right-hand greenside bunker out of play, but there are recovery problems either side of the narrow green for a shot missing the target.

Even a good drive at the 17th hole can leave the ball in an uneven lie among the humps and hollows.

the realms of what-might-have-been, Harry Bradshaw's decision to play his ball out of a broken beer bottle in which it lodged instead of taking a penalty drop, during the second round of the 1949 championship, must rank among the most haunting. He took a double bogey and eventually tied with Bobby Locke, who beat him for the title in a 36-hole playoff.

Perhaps the true secret of success at Royal St George's is to seize the moment when the prospect of success swings tantalisingly close. This was clearly the moment for Greg Norman in 1993, when he dwarfed the entire field with a last-round 64 to win the title in the presence of the venerable Gene Sarazen, the first man to achieve the Grand Slam of four major titles, who declared, "I never thought I'd live to see golf played so well."

The defining link between ancient and modern can be traced to Henry Cotton's victory in 1934, when he was so far ahead of his rivals that the fans regarded his final round as a lap of honour. Not so. He toiled over the first nine holes in 40 strokes and seemed doomed

to throw it all away. Even J H Taylor, the 1894 champion, who followed him as a spectator, was seen "poking his arms to the right" to show how Cotton should be playing the shots in a right-hand crosswind.

Yet Cotton steadied himself and came back to win by five strokes and be hailed as the hero who had at last broken the 10-year American monopoly of the trophy. There was, however, a poignant postscript to his victory. For two rounds he had spotted the frail figure of Harry Vardon, twice champion at Sandwich, sitting at the Maiden short hole, but on the final day the great man was too ill to leave the nearby Guilford Hotel.

Afterwards Cotton went there, entered his room, and without a word handed over the claret jug. Vardon began to weep. Perhaps it was the joy at meeting an old friend, for this trophy had been his for six years. Perhaps it was a reminder of glories past and the great names that had been part of his life and of the infirmities that now trapped him. Cotton also wept. For him it was a beginning. And Vardon knew that too.

Exempt Competitors

Name, Country	Category
Robert Allenby, Australia	4, 14
Stuart Appleby, Australia	1, 4
Paul Azinger, USA	18
*Ricky Barnes, USA	29
Rich Beem, USA	4, 12, 14
Thomas Bjorn, Denmark	1, 4, 5, 18
Tom Byrum, USA	17
Angel Cabrera, Argentina	4, 5
Mark Calcavecchia, USA	3, 18
Chad Campbell, USA	15
Michael Campbell, New Zealand	4, 5
Paul Casey, England	4
K J Choi, Korea	4, 14
Stewart Cink, USA	18
Darren Clarke, N Ireland	4, 18
Jose Coceres, Argentina	17
Fred Couples, USA	4
Ben Curtis, USA	17
John Daly, USA	2
Brian Davis, England	7
Robert-Jan Derksen, Netherlands	7
Chris DiMarco, USA	4, 14
Luke Donald, England	17
Bradley Dredge, Wales	5
Joe Durant, USA	16
David Duval, USA	2, 18
Steve Elkington, Australia	1
Ernie Els, South Africa	1, 4, 5, 10, 14
Bob Estes, USA	4
Gary Evans, England	1
Nick Faldo, England	3, 11
Niclas Fasth, Sweden	4, 5, 18
Brad Faxon, USA	5
Kenneth Ferrie, England	7
Steve Flesch, USA	4
Alastair Forsyth, Scotland	8
Mark Foster, England	24
Pierre Fulke, Sweden	18
Fred Funk, USA	4, 14
Jim Furyk, USA	4, 10, 14, 18
Sergio Garcia, Spain	1, 4, 5, 14, 18
Ignacio Garrido, Spain	6
Philip Golding, England	8
Retief Goosen, South Africa	1, 4, 5, 10, 14
Mathias Gronberg, Sweden	7
Jay Haas, USA	4

Name, Country	Category
Todd Hamilton, USA	25
Anders Hansen, Denmark	5, 6
Soren Hansen, Denmark	1, 5
Padraig Harrington, Ireland	1, 4, 5, 18
Dudley Hart, USA	17
S K Ho, Korea	26
Charles Howell III, USA	4, 14
David Howell, England	8
Trevor Immelman, South Africa	4, 5, 24
Fredrik Jacobson, Sweden	7
Raphael Jacquelin, France	9
Lee Janzen, USA	10
Shingo Katayama, Japan	23
Jonathan Kaye, USA	16
Jerry Kelly, USA	4, 14
Skip Kendell, USA	17
Soren Kjeldsen, Denmark	8
Cliff Kresge, USA	16
Bernhard Langer, Germany	4, 5, 18
Paul Lawrie, Scotland	2, 4, 5
Stephen Leaney, Australia	5
Tom Lehman, USA	2
Justin Leonard, USA	1, 2, 4, 14
Thomas Levet, France	1
J L Lewis, USA	16
Peter Lonard, Australia	1, 4, 22
Davis Love III, USA	1, 4, 13, 18
Sandy Lyle, Scotland	3
David Lynn, England	9
Shigeki Maruyama, Japan	1, 4, 14

It's a Fact

Jack White was the first to record an aggregate for 72 holes of under 300, with his 296 in 1904 in the Open Championship at Royal St George's. This came with the advent of the rubber-cored Haskell ball, which changed the game. The 1904 Open was also the first in which scores under 70 were recorded, 68 by J H Taylor in the fourth round, 69 by James Braid in the third round, and 69 by White in the fourth round.

Name, Country	Category	Name, Country	Category
Len Mattiace, USA	4, 14	Mark Roe, England	9
Scott McCarron, USA	17	John Rollins, USA	19
Paul McGinley, Ireland	18	Eduardo Romero, Argentina	4, 5
Mark McNulty, Zimbabwe	8	Justin Rose, England	4, 5
Phil Mickelson, USA	4, 14, 18	Rory Sabbatini, South Africa	16
Hirofumi Miyase, Japan	26	Nobuhito Sato, Japan	23
Colin Montgomerie, Scotland	4, 5, 6, 18	Charl Schwartzel, South Africa	9
Rolf Muntz, Netherlands	9	Adam Scott, Australia	4, 5
Gary Murphy, Ireland	9	Vijay Singh, Fiji	4, 11, 12, 14
Greg Norman, Australia	2	Jeff Sluman, USA	4, 14
Nick O'Hern, Australia	9	David Smail, New Zealand	20
Jose Maria Olazabal, Spain	5, 11	Chris Smith, USA	17
Andrew Oldcorn, Scotland	6	Noboru Sugai, Japan	27
Peter O'Malley, Australia	1, 22	Hal Sutton, USA	13, 18
Mark O'Meara, USA	2	Toru Taniguchi, Japan	23
Greg Owen, England	8	Hideto Tanihara, Japan	26
Jesper Parnevik, Sweden	18	Katsuyoshi Tomori, Japan	26
Craig Parry, Australia	4, 22	David Toms, USA	4, 12, 14, 18
Corey Pavin, USA	10	Scott Verplank, USA	4, 18
Craig Perks, New Zealand	13	Duffy Waldorf, USA	16
Kenny Perry, USA	4	Tom Watson, USA	3
Ian Poulter, England	8	Mike Weir, Canada	4, 11
Nick Price, Zimbabwe	1, 2, 4, 14	Lee Westwood, England	18
Phillip Price, Wales	18	*Gary Wolstenholme, England	28
Iain Pyman, England	9	Tiger Woods, USA	2, 4, 10, 11, 12, 13, 14, 18
Jyoti Randhawa, India	21		
Chris Riley, USA	4	* Denotes amateurs	

Final Qualifiers

Littlestone
Steven Bowditch, Australia, 65-70–135
Paul Wesselingh, England, 72-64–136
Adam Le Vesconte, Australia, 68-68–136
Christopher Smith, USA, 68-69–137
Robert Coles, England, 68-69–137
*Scott Godfrey, England, 69-69–138
(P) Anthony Wall, England, 70-70–140

North Foreland
Hennie Otto, South Africa, 65-63–128
Andrew George, England, 69-63–132
Adam Mednick, Sweden, 67-65–132
Gary Emerson, England, 65-67–132
Anthony Sproston, England, 68-65–133
Simon Wakefield, England, 61-72–133
(P) Marten Olander, Sweden, 67-67–134

Prince's
Jarrod Moseley, Australia, 70–66–136
Steen Tinning, Denmark, 66-70–136
Andrew Raitt, England, 69–68–137
Marco Ruiz, Paraguay, 69-70–139
(P) Ian Woosnam, Wales, 70-70–140
(P) Cameron Percy, Australia, 73–67–140
(P) Mathew Goggin, Australia, 71–69–140

Royal Cinque Ports
Mark Smith, England, 69-66–135
Ben Crane, USA, 70-66–136
Malcolm Mackenzie, England, 70-69–139
Markus Brier, Austria, 69-70–139
(P) Peter Fowler, Australia, 71-69–140
(P) Charles Challen, England, 73-67–140
(P) Euan Little, Scotland, 73-67–140

* Denotes amateurs   (P) Qualified after playoff

Key to Exemptions from Regional and Final Qualifying

Exemptions for 2003 were granted to the following:

(1) First 15 and anyone tying for 15th place in the 2002 Open Championship.

(2) The Open Champions 1993-2002.

(3) Past Open Champions aged 65 or under on 20 July 2003.

(4) The first 50 players on the Official World Golf Ranking as at 29 May 2003.

(5) First 20 in the PGA European Tour Final Volvo Order of Merit for 2002.

(6) The Volvo PGA Champions for 2000-2003.

(7) First 5 and anyone tying for 5th place, not otherwise exempt, in the top 20 of the PGA European Tour Final Volvo Order of Merit for 2003 at 29 May.

(8) First 7 European Tour members and any European Tour member tying for 7th place, not otherwise exempt, in the top 25 of a cumulative money list taken from all official PGA European Tour events from the Volvo PGA Championship up to and including the Barclays Scottish Open.

(9) The leading 8 players not otherwise exempt having applied (8) above, in the 2003 Barclays Scottish Open. Ties for last place or places will be decided by the better final round score and, if still tied, by the better third round score and then by the better second round score. If still tied, all players thus still tying will be deemed exempt under this category.

Note: Players who appeared in the draw for Rounds 3 and 4 of the 2003 Barclays Scottish Open were ineligible to compete in the Final Qualifying Competition.

(10) The US Open Champions for 1994-2003.

(11) The US Masters Champions for 1999-2003.

(12) The USPGA Champions for 1998-2002.

(13) The USPGA Tour Players Champions for 2000-2003.

(14) First 20 on the Official Money List of the USPGA Tour for 2002.

(15) First 5 and anyone tying for 5th place, not otherwise exempt, in the top 20 of the Official Money List of the USPGA Tour for 2003 at 29 May.

(16) First 7 USPGA Tour members and any USPGA Tour member tying for 7th place, not otherwise exempt, in the top 25 of a cumulative money list taken from the USPGA Tour Players Championship and the 5 USPGA Tour events leading up to and including the 100th Western Open.

(17) The leading 8 players not otherwise exempt having applied (16) above, in the 100th Western Open. Ties for last place or places will be decided by the better final round score and, if still tied, by the better third round score and then by the better second round score. If still tied, all players thus still tying will be deemed exempt under this category.

(18) Playing members of the 2002 Ryder Cup teams.

(19) The Canadian Open Champion for 2002.

(20) The Japan Open Champion for 2002.

(21) First place on the Asian PGA Davidoff Tour for 2002.

(22) First 3 and anyone tying for 3rd place on the Tour of Australasia for 2002/2003.

(23) First 3 and anyone tying for 3rd place on the Japan Golf Tour for 2002.

(24) First 2 and anyone tying for 2nd place on the Southern Africa PGA Sunshine Tour for 2002/2003.

(25) The leading player, not otherwise exempt, in the 2003 Mizuno Open.

(26) First 4 and anyone tying for 4th place, who are not otherwise exempt having applied (25) above, in the top 20 of a cumulative money list taken from all official Japan Golf Tour events from the Japan PGA Championship up to and including the Mizuno Open.

(27) The Senior British Open Champion for 2002.

(28) The Amateur Champion for 2003.

(29) The US Amateur Champion for 2002.

(30) The European Individual Amateur Champion for 2002.

Note: Exemption for performance as an amateur under (28) to (30) inclusive would only be granted if the entrant concerned was still an amateur on 17 July 2003.

First Round

What If Hogan Were Here?

By Robert Sommers

Through meticulous planning, the great Ben Hogan built a reputation as a master tactician.

Arriving at every venue a week or more before his first competitive round, Hogan studied the course so thoroughly he seemed to know every level spot on every fairway, where to place his drive for the best approach to the green, and where to place his approach to assure, first, that it would stay there and, second, that he would have a reasonable chance to hole the putt. If by chance his approach settled in a bunker, he left the impression that, well, that's probably the best way to play the hole.

Those who remembered Hogan and who witnessed the 2003 Open Championship were led to wonder just how Ben would have handled Royal St George's, how he could have protected against the wild and unpredictable bounces so much a part of this brutally hard course that deflected well-struck drives into occasionally knee-high grass, and where he would ever find a flat area on this tumbling linksland.

Ten years after his victory, Greg Norman was on his game.

Royal St George's had been revised after the 1993 Open field made par an irrelevant figure. New tees had been added, the course lengthened, and after a dry, hot summer, the fairways had turned hard as a blacksmith's anvil. It had become, truly, a man-sized course. It tested the imagination, the shot-making skills, and the patience of the world's premier players. It surprised them as well.

Tiger Woods, who stepped onto the first tee of every tournament expecting to win, opened with a 7 on a par-4 hole; Jerry Kelly shot 11 on the same hole; 48-year-old Greg Norman, playing in only his third tournament of the year, shot 69. Ernie Els began his defense of his 2002 championship with a poor 78; both Jim Furyk, the US Open champion, and Mike Weir, who won the Masters, shot 74s; Steve Elkington, a loser in the 2002 playoff, shot 86 and gave up, and Colin Montgomerie fell down, hurt his hand, and withdrew on the eighth hole.

At the end of the day, the field looked up and saw Hennie Otto in first place. A 27-year-old South African who preferred rugby but devoted himself to golf because that was where the money was, Otto returned a steady 68, three under par on a course where hold-

1

First Round • 21

THURSDAY WEATHER
Scattered showers in the morning,
SW winds throughout the day.

The rumpled ground of Royal St George's caused problems for all.

ing a ball on a fairway could be the most difficult problem facing the field.

In Royal St George's, the players found an insoluble dilemma. The ground heaves and rolls, humps appear from nowhere, often kicking the ball sideways towards the rough, which at its worst could rip the club from the hands.

Statistics show that Woods hit only three fairways during the first round, but those figures are misleading. His drives often caught safe ground but took unexpected bounces either right or left and settled in rough grass. At the end of the four rounds, those same statistics say he hit only half the fairways, but again, good shots brought poor results. It worked the same for everyone.

Furthermore, the weather that first day began rainy and ended windy. A freshening breeze swept in from the southwest at a force of between 20 and 25 miles an hour, often gusting to 30 or 35. Players unfamiliar with the course found the wind as troubling as those capricious bounces.

Norman talked of often aiming at a spot 30 or 40 yards right or left of a fairway and allowing the wind to sweep the ball back into play. Some younger players struggled to force themselves to take such risks, but it

---

Davis Love III did not have a bogey until the last hole.

First Round Leaders

HOLE	1	2	3	4	5	6	7	8	9	10	11	12	13	14	15	16	17	18	
PAR	4	4	3	5	4	3	5	4	4	4	3	4	4	5	4	3	4	4	TOTAL
Hennie Otto	4	4	[4]	5	4	3	(4)	(3)	4	(3)	3	(3)	(3)	5	4	3	4	[5]	68
Davis Love III	(3)	4	3	(4)	4	3	5	4	4	4	3	4	4	5	4	3	(3)	[5]	69
Greg Norman	(3)	4	3	(3)	4	3	5	4	4	4	(2)	4	4	[6]	4	3	4	[5]	69
S K Ho	[5]	4	[4]	(4)	4	3	(4)	[5]	(3)	4	3	(3)	4	[6]	(3)	3	4	4	70
Fredrik Jacobson	4	4	3	(4)	4	3	5	4	4	4	3	4	5	4	3	4	4		70
Gary Evans	4	[5]	3	(4)	4	[4]	(4)	[5]	4	4	3	(3)	(3)	(4)	[5]	3	[5]	4	71
Tom Watson	(3)	4	3	(4)	4	3	5	[5]	(3)	4	3	4	4	5	4	(2)	[6]	[5]	71
Fred Couples	4	(3)	3	(4)	[5]	(2)	5	4	4	4	3	4	[5]	5	4	3	[5]	4	71
Charles Howell III	4	[5]	3	5	4	3	5	(3)	4	4	[4]	(3)	4	5	4	3	4	4	71
Thomas Levet	4	4	3	(4)	4	3	5	(3)	4	4	3	4	4	5	[5]	3	[5]	4	71
Mathias Gronberg	4	4	3	(4)	4	3	(4)	4	4	4	3	(3)	4	5	4	[4]	[5]	[5]	71
Scott McCarron	4	4	3	5	4	3	[6]	4	4	[5]	(2)	(3)	[5]	5	4	3	(3)	4	71

Korean S K Ho was "very happy to make under par."

In his first Open round ever, Hennie Otto posted five birdies.

worked for Norman, who had played through these conditions for many years.

As a consequence, only five players scored under par. Aside from Otto, at 68, and Norman, at 69, Davis Love III played a steady round with three birdies and a lost stroke only on the 18th and matched Norman's 69. S K Ho, a slender, 29-year-old Korean who would hang around until the end, and the Swede Fredrik Jacobson shot 70.

Seven others matched par 71, and six more shot 72, among them a 26-year-old former Ohio Amateur champion, Ben Curtis, a total stranger to big-time golf.

Woods finished among the 16 men who shot 73 and caused the biggest stir of the day when he played his first drive so poorly it veered off to the right, sailed over the heads of forecaddies and marshals alike, burrowed into deep, nearly knee-high grass, and remained there until another marshal stepped on it hours later. Woods believed it was the first time he had lost a ball during his professional career.

Driven back to the tee in a buggy, Woods played another drive equally bad but found it, hacked it across the fairway into a playable position in the left rough, pitched onto the green, and two-putted from 15 feet for his 7.

Never giving up, he played the rest of the holes in one under par, still in the championship.

Kelly couldn't say the same. He, too, drove into the rough but on the left, moved his first recovery attempt about 15 feet, played his next shot sideways simply to escape but flew it into deeper rough on the right, took four more hacks that barely moved the ball, took relief for an unplayable ball, and dropped into a position where he could at least play a shot. Still, he missed the green to the left, played a loose chip that left him 30 feet from the hole, then saved his 11 by holing the putt.

Sometime during all that heavy work, Kelly damaged a finger and withdrew after posting an 86.

Kelly, of course, at least played a full round. Montgomerie didn't get that far. Leaving earlier in the day

Fredrik Jacobson returned a 70 without dropping a shot.

Gary Evans made three successive birdies from the 12th.

Low Scores

Low First Nine
Greg Norman — 33

Low Second Nine
Hennie Otto — 33

Low Round
Hennie Otto — 68

Despite a 74, Phil Mickelson said it was a "fun" day.

Monty
Tumbles Out

Two days before the off, Colin Montgomerie, who attracts more than his share of an Open crowd, had been asked how he rated his chances in the Open on a scale of one to 10. "If I didn't say 10," said Montgomerie with, it has to be said, rather less than his usual aplomb, "I shouldn't be here."

In truth, the 40-year-old Scot's confidence had taken a bit of a knock with his 53rd place in the Barclays Scottish Open at Loch Lomond the week before. Yet his preparation at Royal St George's had been encouraging, with Denis Pugh, his coach, and Hugh Mantle, his psychologist, agreeing that if he were to set off on the right foot, he could have a useful week.

Far from setting off on the right foot, Montgomerie tripped over a step and fell heavily onto gravel in the hotel courtyard some four and a half hours before his tee-off time. His right thumb bore the brunt of the fall and, though he made light of it over breakfast with Pugh, his coach sensed the worst. "I knew things were serious when he had trouble eating his breakfast," Pugh said.

The problems Montgomerie was having with his knife and fork were mirrored with his golfing irons. With his hand having swollen, he struggled to find a comfortable hold on the club and hit no more than a handful of practice shots. "I went ahead only because of my competitive nature and because this was the Open," Montgomerie said.

Out on the course, Montgomerie dropped a shot at each of the first two holes and knew the end was nigh when his improvised grip resulted in a shank from the sixth tee. He called it a day at the eighth after driving into the rough, the mere sight of which made him wince. A buggy was dispatched to pick him up and R&A medical men had no difficulty in understanding why he could go no further.

So brave a face did the Scot put on this golfing setback that some thought he did not care enough.

The three painkillers Montgomerie had taken at the start of the day had maybe had their effect on rather more than merely his thumb. Only gradually would he be hit by the full force of what it meant to miss out on an Open at this relatively late stage in his career. "It's been a desperately disappointing Open for him," said his manager, Guy Kinnings.

While others were able to pursue their Open dream, a distraught Montgomerie headed for his Surrey home and a series of x-rays. There were no bones broken but there was serious soft tissue damage, specifically to the carpal ligament, which called for some physiotherapy.

—*Lewine Mair*

to have breakfast, he stepped out of his hotel, looked up as he felt rain, tripped over a step, fell, and injured his right thumb and wrist badly. He tried to play, but he quit when he felt he might cause more damage if he continued.

It was a frustrating end to another of Monty's failed attempts to win one of the game's great prizes.

Montgomerie's accident happened at about 7.30 Thursday morning. By then, Otto had been on the course for an hour. He had climbed out of bed at 4 o'clock to make his 6.30 starting time. Grouped with Iain Pyman and Chris Smith, two players from Britain, they made up the first group off the tee.

A regular on the PGA European Tour, Otto had shown himself to be a bit of an eccentric. During a tournament once in South Africa, he had become so disgusted with his game he had sneaked off to a riverbank where no one could see him, dumped all his clubs

Tom Watson was having a fine summer.

With 71, Fred Couples "thought I would do better."

from his bag, one by one snapped each shaft over his knee, then flung them all into the swirling current. They would never betray him again. Later he was warned that he should be fined, but because he had done the deed in solitude, he would escape the Southern African Tour's wrath.

Otto showed no such display of frustration this day, even though he looked as if he might fall to two over par after four holes. After opening with two pars, Otto stood at the tee of the third, a 210-yard par 3, ripped into a three iron that missed the green, chipped to four feet, and missed the putt. A bogey 4; on to the fourth, a shortish par 5 of just 497 yards.

The drive here must carry a giant knoll scarred by a deep bunker measuring at least 25 feet from top to bottom carved into its face. It was here in 1979 where Reg Glading lost the English Amateur on the fourth extra hole when he climbed to the top of the bunker to play his ball and tumbled to the bottom when the sand gave way. His ball and club followed him down,

His 71 was a welcome start for the Swede Mathias Gronberg, who had missed the cut in four previous Opens.

and when he stopped rolling he had violated more rules of golf than either he or his opponent could count.

No one in the Open experienced such an adventure, and Otto's drive cleared the summit easily, but dived into the rough. From this lie, Otto felt he might not reach the green, and so he determined that if he missed he would miss to the right, because during practice rounds he had worked on his chipping from the right. Sure enough, he missed on the right, chipped on, took two putts and made his par.

Still one over through the sixth, Otto birdied five of the next seven holes and moved to four under par. He picked up his first birdie on the

Scott McCarron tried to be patient.

My Favourite
Open

1967 HOYLAKE

Donald Steel
Golf Course Architect

"Roberto de Vicenzo had been a favourite of mine. I liked the way he played, like all of us would like to play. Everybody in the world was delighted he won, because he was such a wonderful guy."

Stephen Leaney was runner-up in the US Open.

Thomas Levet bogeyed two of the last four holes.

Sergio Garcia (above) was two under par after 11 holes. Ian Woosnam (below) came through qualifying.

Gary Wolstenholme shot 74.

Charles Howell III played the last seven holes in one under par.

Until today, Tiger Woods had never lost a golf ball as a professional.

seventh, a 532-yard par 5, where he drove with a three wood, followed with a two iron, then chipped and putted for the 4, and played a drive and three iron to the eighth and holed from 25 feet.

Out in 35, one under par, Otto birdied the 10th, 12th, and 13th, holing 30-foot putts on the last two.

That was the end of his streak, and while he parred every hole through the 17th, Otto dropped one stroke on the 18th, where his four iron from the right rough pulled up short of the home green, and he missed from eight feet.

Still, Otto had set the standard for the day, and no one matched it.

Certainly not Woods, although, as always, he never gave up, and indeed struck back with birdies on the fourth and 10th. Just one over par now, he threw away strokes from the 12th through the 14th, again because of loose driving. He drove into fairway bunkers on both the 12th and 13th and couldn't reach the green, then into the gallery on the 14th, another par 5, and took four strokes to get on. He two-putted each hole.

Now he stood four over par with four holes to play. Once again he struck back. His putting had not been up to the standard everyone had expected of him; he had seldom left himself within reasonable birdie range, and when he did, his ball glanced at the hole as it glided past, or else pulled up short. Now on the 15th he looked like the Tiger of old,

In the Words of the Competitors...

"

"Yes, I hit some bad drives, but I also hit some really good ones that landed in the middle of the fairway and went in the rough."

—Tiger Woods

"I wanted to play rugby, but golf is where the money is."

—Hennie Otto

"There was not an easy shot out there today. The golf course was there, baring her teeth all the way round. I'm glad it rained a little bit overnight and softened it up."

—Greg Norman

"It's been a good summer but it's been bitter sweet because my caddie (Bruce Edwards) has a terrible disease (Amyotrophic Lateral Sclerosis) that is wasting his body away and he couldn't make the trip, but he was here in spirit."

—Tom Watson

"I felt I didn't deserve four bogeys on the last six, given the way I hit the ball, but that's the way the Open is."

—Sergio Garcia

"You have to use your imagination out there a lot. ... I would say your experience comes into play."

—Ian Woosnam

"

Donald Takes Centre Stage

One of the most high octane groups of the first two rounds comprised Luke Donald, one of the brightest young things in golf in Europe and a rising star on the US circuit, and Sergio Garcia as Tiger Woods's playing companions. Donald had been a star for Great Britain and Ireland in the victorious 1999 and 2001 Walker Cup, winning seven of his eight matches, and then had won a tournament on his debut season in the US. As a mark of his success he had been chosen to be one of the team advertising the Royal Bank of Scotland and one of another team selling the wares of Ralph Lauren.

It is rare that Woods is the oldest member of his group, but at 27 Woods could give four years to Garcia and two to Donald. Woods was pleased with the draw when he discovered it on Tuesday afternoon. "Hmmm," he said. "9.09 and 2.05. That's cool." He was asked whether he had played with Donald before. "Don't think so," Woods replied. "I've had lunch with him a few times though."

It is an enormous compliment to be paired with the world's best player, yet it also brings its own pressures. Donald knew that he had to be patient to cope with the stress attendant upon playing with Woods as well as coping with the course's irregular and irrational bounces. The former was unique to playing with Woods, the latter liable to occur to anyone playing Royal St George's. Of the Open courses, Royal Lytham has more bunkers, Carnoustie may be harder, and the Old Course is older and more historic. But none of these has fairways that are as rumpled as St George's. Sometimes when you stand on a tee and look at the landing area for a drive, you could be mistaken for thinking you were trying to land a ball on a rumpled eiderdown.

If as he contemplated the first two days Donald needed a reference point, then he had only to look back one year and see that Justin Rose had been paired with Woods for the first two rounds at Muirfield in 2002, and though Rose had been outscored by five strokes after two rounds, he overtook Woods and finished one stroke ahead after four rounds.

"I am excited about playing with Tiger," Donald had said on Tuesday. "This is what I play for. I look forward to getting into pressure situations and competing against the best. It is good experience for me and a big chance. My coach is here, I am looking forward to it."

For 16 holes Donald looked as though he was making the most of it. He had recovered from a nervous start when he dropped strokes on both the first and second holes and was two under par for the run of holes starting at the 12th and ending at the 16th. That made him one over par overall. Woods, alongside Donald, had been much worse than that, soaring to three over par after the first, where he lost a ball, and was back to four over par after the 14th. But whereas Woods then birdied the 15th and the 16th and parred the last two holes, Donald showed his inexperience and finished limply. He tried to be too ambitious from a greenside bunker on the penultimate hole and ran up a 6. On the 18th he hit a poor drive down the left, found his ball in a bad lie, and took three to reach the green, whereupon he three-putted for another 6. A 76, five over par, was not the way he would have wanted to start, and as it happened, he would not play on the weekend.

—*John Hopkins*

Luke Donald's 6, 6 finish spoilt his round.

running in a putt from 40 feet or more, and another from just inside 20 feet on the 16th.

When he closed with par 4s on the last two, he had come back in 35 after a grim outward 38. Still, his 73 left him within range of the leaders.

Ernie Els, though, was another matter. This Open had promised to develop into a battle between Els, the defender, and Woods, who everyone acknowledged as the best player in the game. For his part, Els had looked especially sharp in winning the Barclays Scottish Open the week before the Open, his third victory of the year on the European Tour, and he had won twice on the USPGA Tour, both early in the season. He had also

Ernie Els never quite had control of his shots.

Round of the Day

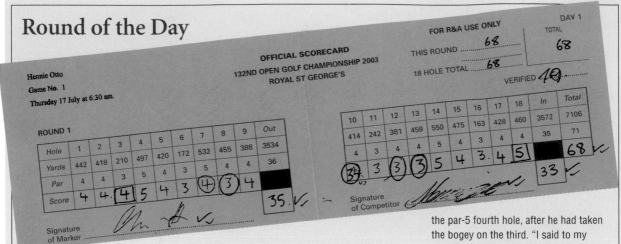

In the first round of his first Open Championship, Hennie Otto returned the low score of the day with 68, three under par. He made bogeys on the third and 18th holes and five birdies in between. Aged 27 and a six-times winner in his native South Africa and on the European Challenge Tour, Otto turned professional in 1997 and joined the PGA European Tour in 1999. He led this year's Open final qualifying at North Foreland with rounds of 65 and 63, and was in the first game of the championship, off at 6.30 a.m.

A key to Otto's first-round score was a chip to the green and a par-saving putt on the par-5 fourth hole, after he had taken the bogey on the third. "I said to my caddie, if we miss, we miss to the right, and I can always chip it back on," Otto said. He chipped and putted for a birdie on the par-5 seventh, and holed putts of between 25 and 30 feet for birdies on the eighth, 12th, and 13th holes. His four-iron approach to the 18th was short of the green, and he missed a try for par from eight feet.

My Favourite *Open*

1966 MUIRFIELD

Jack Nicklaus
Open Champion
1966, 1970, 1978

"My win was so significant (his first in the Open) and the venue so special, when I built my home club in Ohio, I named it Muirfield Village Golf Club."

Hennie Otto was off in Game 1.

handled the bad weather better than Woods during the 2002 Open, shooting 72 in the appalling weather of the third round at Muirfield just after Woods turned in an 81.

Woods and Els practically passed each other—Woods coming in, Els starting out at 1.54, grouped with David Toms, the former USPGA champion, and Shigeki Maruyama, the good-humoured Japanese player who tied for fifth last year at Muirfield. All three played dismal golf. Maruyama shot 83 and Toms played only slightly better, shooting 80. Neither figured in the championship.

Greeted by enthusiastic applause at his introduction, Els played loose golf from the start. He drove into the rough, his second reached the green but his 40-foot putt died far short of the hole, and he missed the second putt.

Throughout the day Els never quite had control of his shots. Once again his drive found the left rough on the second hole, his approach rolled onto the back fringe, and he got down in two for his par.

"It was a tough day," said Tiger Woods (above), "but I kept my patience and grinded my way around this golf course."

Kenny Perry, at age 42, was playing in only his second Open, but was having a dream summer with three wins.

Greg Norman
10 Years Later

By Mike Aitken

It was as if the 10 years which had elapsed since Greg Norman signed for 64 at Royal St George's to raise the claret jug for a second time were a mere 10 hours, and the Great White Shark simply carried on where he'd left off at the 1993 Open Championship. Although there's no public record of Norman keeping a time machine at his home in Jupiter, Florida, alongside his private jet, helicopter, racing cars, and ocean yacht, the Australian's sparkling first round of 69 whisked his game back to the future.

As his blond hair, now shorter, fell beneath a dark baseball cap and his tanned, chiselled features peered down the first fairway, it looked for all the world as if Norman, the champion golfer the last time the Open was held in Kent, had discovered the secret of turning back the clock. It was an impression confirmed by a glorious birdie on the opening hole made all the more astonishing by the knowledge Tiger Woods would start the day with a triple-bogey 7 and Jerry Kelly lost the plot altogether with an 11.

The story of Norman's return to prominence on the world stage at the site of a past triumph had begun weeks earlier with a return to practice in Florida under the coaching of Rick Smith after being sidelined from competition for much of the year through a combination of back trouble and business commitments.

His preparations for the championship were completed in the north of Scotland on the links at Royal Dornoch the weekend prior to the championship by playing golf with friends. When he teed up in Sandwich for only his third tournament appearance of the season, Norman was sufficiently re-acquainted with the shot-making skills required to thrive on the seaside courses of the British Isles.

Although Norman's career in America, where he was unable to win any of the three major championships staged on the other side of the Atlantic, is often interpreted in a bittersweet fashion, a tale of what might have been, his legacy in the Open is glorious.

In 1993, for example, the leaderboard on the last day was peerless. Virtually all of the best players in the world at the time were playing at the highest level. Norman, as it turned out, was too good for Nick Faldo, shooting 64 in the closing round to hold off a chasing pack which also included Bernhard Langer and Corey Pavin.

"When I look back on that tournament," Norman reminisced, "it was obviously one of the greatest tournaments I ever played, irrespective of whether I won or not. In every interview I've ever given I've always said I never played in another tournament where so many of the world's great players were in contention. There were 12 or 13 guys going into that final round on Sunday within four or five shots of the lead. I knew that a Faldo-like round of 18 pars would never work in the last round of that Open. I needed to go low and fortunately I did."

A decade later and Norman has made the transition from champion to entrepreneur more successfully than any other player. He says golf is still a priority but no longer his number one priority. No one has yet forgotten Norman, but he admitted he was able to come in under the radar at Royal St George's.

His 69, one of only five scores below par on the first day, came about because Norman was able to delve into the memory bank and call on the techniques he had mastered to win on the links at Turnberry in 1986 (where he shot 63, the round of his career) as well as at Royal St George's. At age 48, it wasn't a case of living in the past and remembering old glories. Norman knew he could still resemble a master of the seaside universe.

For all his success on the course, Norman conceded Sandwich had never won his heart. The combination of blind shots and odd nuances made the links too quirky to be a favourite. But he acknowledged the severity of the challenge posed by firm and fast fairways.

Norman also attributed his two-under-par flourish to an enduring gift for the ancient game. He hit a number of bump-and-run shots with a four iron and spoke of his love of seaside golf. On the fourth he recalled having four options to get to the green and was able to picture the shot in his mind without needing to know the yardage.

There was also a thrilling two iron from an upslope on the 17th fairway which was similarly intuitive and scuttled over 200 yards to the green. "Outside of the driver, I pretty much punched every other shot I played all day long," he explained. "I enjoy hitting the ball on the ground and chasing it round the golf course. Links golf excites me."

Although his putting deserted him after that electrifying start, the overture was a welcome glimpse on a rare competitive outing of how Norman blended imagination with power. His best golf, as happened 10 years earlier, was as thrilling as anyone's.

Whether or not he should have won more major titles is a debate which leaves such a fulfilled individual untroubled. "You can never tell what life is going to throw you," he admitted. "I've structured my life in such a way where a lot of other great things have happened which transcended winning major championships."

Sandwich was a reminder that he played some great stuff as well.

Starting among the favourites, Vijay Singh (left) and Padraig Harrington returned 75s.

Two more pars brought him to the fifth, a par 4 of 420 yards. Here he looked as if he might have come to life. With the wind at his back, Els ripped into a drive that almost reached the green, so close that with some sharp play a birdie seemed certain. But as usual this day, instead of a birdie, Els walked away with a par 4.

And so it went. With the eighth playing into the full strength of the wind, Els drove into the right rough, pushed his approach even farther right, pitched on and rammed his putt against the back of the hole. Of course, it didn't fall.

Out in 40, Els started back with a string of three-putt greens, played the second nine in 38, and at the end of his first round found himself 10 strokes behind another South African few at Sandwich had ever heard of before noon.

Els's shabby play couldn't be compared to Greg Norman's intelligent attacking golf. Returning to the site of his second Open Championship, which he had won 10 years earlier, Norman played much as he had back in 1993—controlling the ball, never flailing carelessly, and always keeping the ball in play. He kept his shots low to bore through the wind, not allowing his ball to soar high enough to be blown into deep trouble.

His play on the fourth offered a prime example. Safely past the knoll and its treacherous bunker, Norman's ball sat in the fairway below the level of the green with the wind coming at him. Hardly hesitating, he drew out his four iron, played another low shot that hit short of the green, scooted on directly at the flagstick, and stopped less than a foot

In the Words of the Competitors...

"

"It was a real problem with my putting, and I threw away a lot of shots on the greens early in the round."

—Ernie Els

"I wouldn't mind being the first Swedish golfer to win a major, and that's what I'm trying for."

—Fredrik Jacobson

"Before coming to play here, I only wanted to learn from the world top players. If I can play like today and until Sunday, I am going to be so nervous."

—S K Ho

"If you hit it in the wrong place, you are going to pay the price."

—Davis Love III

"I played the easy holes very well and I struggled on the harder holes, and I scored a decent round to be in contention."

—Phil Mickelson

"I am disappointed that I left several shots out there. Yesterday I would have taken 74 but I felt my golf deserved 71."

—Gary Wolstenholme

"It was mega-tough today. Under par would be a hell of a score."

—Paul Lawrie

"

Round One Hole Summary

HOLE	PAR	EAGLES	BIRDIES	PARS	BOGEYS	D. BOGEYS	HIGHER	RANK	AVERAGE
1	4	0	6	90	48	10	2	4	4.46
2	4	1	13	107	31	4	0	13	4.15
3	3	0	6	111	37	2	0	12	3.22
4	5	5	59	70	17	3	2	17	4.75
5	4	0	10	114	32	0	0	14	4.14
6	3	0	7	82	58	9	0	6	3.44
7	5	3	58	81	12	2	0	18	4.69
8	4	0	7	46	73	24	5	1	4.83
9	4	0	15	75	48	14	3	5	4.46
OUT	**36**	**9**	**181**	**776**	**356**	**68**	**12**		**38.16**
10	4	0	8	90	44	9	3	8	4.41
11	3	0	7	102	44	1	0	11	3.25
12	4	0	25	93	31	5	0	16	4.10
13	4	0	11	86	54	2	1	10	4.33
14	5	0	14	79	48	11	2	8	5.41
15	4	0	7	87	49	9	2	7	4.43
16	3	0	18	100	33	3	0	15	3.14
17	4	0	5	70	66	11	2	3	4.58
18	4	0	2	61	75	14	2	2	4.70
IN	**35**	**0**	**97**	**768**	**444**	**65**	**12**		**38.34**
TOTAL	**71**	**9**	**278**	**1544**	**800**	**133**	**24**		**76.50**

short of the hole. An easy eagle 3.

Speaking of the shot later, he said his ball lay 194 yards from the hole, and he had four options.

"I could have hit a five iron, land it on the front of the green and let it one-bounce up and stop; hook it to the front with a six iron; or I could have tried to fly it up on top by cutting a high four iron and hold it against the wind. The only shot that made sense to me was landing it at about 165 to 167 yards and letting it go. It was just a half four-iron shot, really."

Norman had begun his day by punching an eight iron into the first and holing a good putt from about 30 feet, and with the eagle on the fourth, he made the turn in 33, three under par. When he played another four iron to about five feet and birdied the 11th, he moved four under par. If he could hold on, he could shoot 67.

He couldn't. After a poor drive on the 14th, he needed three more shots to reach the green and missed a seven-footer for the par, then rifled a low two iron that pulled up short of the 18th green, chipped on, and again missed from six or seven feet.

Still, Norman had turned in a remarkable round. By 2003 he had reached the age of 48, and furthermore, he had played only two tournaments before arriving at Sandwich. Nor did he seem disappointed by those two late bogeys.

"It was a very difficult day," Norman said. "I don't think there was an easy shot out there. You hit some good shots that land in the middle of the fairway and end up in the rough, and you hit some bad shots that are really bad. You had to be extremely patient.

"If I had been given a 69 before I went to the first tee, I would have more than settled for it. The important thing was the feeling that I could play up to my standard."

It wasn't for lack of effort that Darren Clarke was four over par.

Excerpts from the
Press

"Never mind the Otto Open, this looked very much like a retro Open as first Tom Watson then Greg Norman climbed to prominent positions on the leaderboard. Both led at various stages of the proceedings, as did Davis Love and Freddie Couples, two more Americans with vast experience of this championship."

—Alan Fraser, *Daily Mail*

Alastair Forsyth left Royal St George's cursing the one hole that ruined a glorious Open debut. The Scot had guided himself round the windswept links brilliantly for 16 holes (in level par) but carded a horror 7 at the par-4 17th."

—David McCarthy, *Daily Record*

"The amateur game has instilled in Gary Wolstenholme a delightful grasp of old-fashioned etiquette and courtesy, as we saw when he applauded even more warmly than the people sitting in the grandstand when Mike Weir and Mark O'Meara were announced on the first tee."

—Martin Johnson,
The Daily Telegraph

"Terry Bennett, a 17-handicap member at Royal St George's, achieved what Tiger Woods and dozens of others had failed to do— he found Tiger's lost ball by simply stepping on it."

—David Davies, *The Guardian*

Second Round

Soft Landing Saves Love

By Robert Sommers

Looking seaward across the landscape of Royal St George's Golf Club, a white building stands in the distance. It once served as the clubhouse of the Prince's Golf Club, where long ago Gene Sarazen won his only Open Championship.

The great English amateur Laddie Lucas was born in that building. When war came to Britain in 1939, Lucas joined the RAF and trained as a fighter pilot. Returning from a mission over France, a German fighter swooped down firing and hit Laddie's ammunition drum, setting off an explosion that almost ripped the wing from his Spitfire.

Knowing he couldn't possibly reach his base, Lucas looked down and saw Prince's, banked his plane as best he could, and landed beside the ninth fairway. Safely down, he climbed out, looked around, and said to himself, "I never could hit that fairway."

The old Prince's clubhouse sits directly behind the 14th tee of Royal St George's. In times past, visitors

In his 17th Open, Davis Love III had his first lead.

often mistook it for the first at Prince's. Stay around long enough and you are bound to hear tales of harried Royal St George's club secretaries rushing out to inform perfect strangers that they are playing the wrong course.

Prince's had a new clubhouse by 2003, far from Royal St George's 14th tee, but let your drive leak too far right and the ball could land on the Prince's course—out of bounds. A row of white stakes marks the boundary. Spaced perhaps three or four feet apart, they rise about waist high and run parallel to the hole from the tee well past the green. They turned into a saviour for Davis Love III during the second round.

One stroke behind Hennie Otto after the first round, Love had gone out in 34, two under par, but he had lost all those strokes by bogeying three of the first four holes of the second nine.

Standing on the 14th tee, he had chosen to play safe and drive with a three iron. Moving into the shot with his classic swing, Love stared as his ball started off well enough, but then began drifting right. It came down on a downslope and took a sharp kick towards the out-of-bounds stakes.

2

Excerpts from the *Press*

Sergio Garcia bogeyed the 11th and 12th after hitting into bunkers.

From the tee, Love couldn't follow his ball once it took the kick, but it bounded towards the out-of-bounds stakes, hit one of them, caromed back into safe ground, and settled on a little tuft of grass in the short rough.

Love had had a remarkable stroke of luck. Had his ball slipped between those stakes, he would have had to play another shot from the tee—his third—and most likely score no better than 7. As it was, he made his par 5, finished with 72, and at the end of the day led the Open, at 141, one under par for 36 holes.

Meantime, Otto, the surprising leader of the first round, slipped to 76, and at 144, two over par, dropped to fourth place, along with six others, including that American, Ben Curtis, who, it turned out, had never played in anything quite so important as the Open Championship. Curtis posted a second 72.

Sergio Garcia was in there at 144 too, along with Kenny Perry, the Frenchman Thomas Levet, the Scotsman Alastair Forsyth, and Marco Ruiz, a 28-year-old from Paraguay.

Thomas Bjorn shot 70 and S K Ho shot 73, sharing second place at 143, two strokes behind Love.

Thomas Bjorn was contending despite an 8 on the 17th in the first round.

Players Below Par	9
Players At Par	11
Players Above Par	132

In his first Open, Alastair Forsyth was the leading home player after 36 holes.

Thomas Levet reached three under par then was five over on the last nine.

Without losing a ball, Tiger Woods improved on his first-round score by one bare stroke, returned a 72, and tied Vijay Singh and three others in 11th place, at 145, still only four strokes out of first place. Also in that group were Scott McCarron, Chad Campbell, and Mathias Gronberg.

While Woods seemed stuck in first gear, Ernie Els staged a complete turnaround, improved his first-round score by 10 strokes to 68, the best of the day, and climbed into a 12-man tie for 16th place at 146 that included Phil Mickelson, Nick Price, and Craig Parry. Els not only recorded the best score of the round, only he among the 152-man field scored in the 60s.

Unfortunately, Greg Norman had a sharp turnaround as well. After his almost classic opening round, Norman had nothing left and slipped from 69 to 79. He dropped into a tie for 35th at 148, alongside 12 others including Tom Watson, Ian Woosnam, Padraig Harrington, and Retief Goosen, who two years earlier won the US Open.

The weather had eased from Thursday. Instead of wind gusts of 35 miles an hour, at its strongest it probably hit about 15, still out of the southwest.

Aside from Els, the only man in the 60s, eight others shot 70 and 11 more shot 71—20 men at par or better. Royal St George's remained a severe test of all that determines a champion golfer.

It had also become clear that the scoring must be done on the first nine, because the homeward nine would not surrender birdies easily. Of the 333 birdies given up in the second round, the second nine yielded only 109, and the fourth and seventh yielded all eight eagles, five of them on the seventh.

The course could be beaten, though. Paul Casey, who had opened by shooting 85 in the first round, went out in 31, five under par, but came back in 40, missing the 36-hole cut by six strokes. Scott McCarron shot into the lead briefly by birdieing five holes on the first nine, offset by bogeys on the first two, and shot 33. It all evaporated coming home, though, and McCarron finished with 74, mainly due to a 7 on the 17th.

Hennie Otto, with 76, fell to a tie for fourth place.

Round of the Day

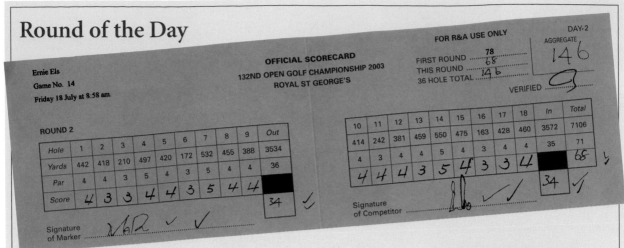

OFFICIAL SCORECARD
132ND OPEN GOLF CHAMPIONSHIP 2003
ROYAL ST GEORGE'S

Ernie Els
Game No. 14
Friday 18 July at 8:58 am.

FOR R&A USE ONLY   DAY·2
                                    AGGREGATE
FIRST ROUND 78   146
THIS ROUND 68
36 HOLE TOTAL 146
                            VERIFIED

ROUND 2

Hole	1	2	3	4	5	6	7	8	9	Out
Yards	442	418	210	497	420	172	532	455	388	3534
Par	4	4	3	5	4	3	5	4	4	36
Score	4	3	3	4	4	3	5	4	4	34

Signature of Marker ......

	10	11	12	13	14	15	16	17	18	In	Total
	414	242	381	459	550	475	163	428	460	3572	7106
	4	3	4	4	5	4	3	4	4	35	71
	4	4	4	3	5	4	3	3	4	34	68

Signature of Competitor ......

Defending champion Ernie Els was in danger of failing to qualify for the final 36 holes when he shot 78, seven over par, in the first round, which left him exactly 100 places from the top of the 156-man field. He remedied that with 68, the low score of the second round, which lifted the South African to a share of 16th place, just five strokes off the lead. "At least I'm here for the week and I've got a chance," Els said.

The turnaround started for Els on the par-4 second hole, where he made birdie from 18 feet. There was a two-putt birdie on the par-5 fourth. "Then I made a mistake on six," Els said. "I only had a wedge into that green and made par, and I was very angry."

Els took bogey 4 after a poor chip on the 11th, but finished with a birdie from eight feet on the par-4 13th and a birdie from 12 feet on the par-4 17th.

"The pin placements are tough, really tough," Els said. "If you get on the wrong side you can only defend on putts. You can't really go out and hit an aggressive putt."

Scott McCarron (right) posted five birdies, five bogeys and 7 on the par-4 17th. Kenny Perry (far right) said he was getting a "crash course" in links golf.

Unlike on the first day, Els began his round early, teeing off two minutes before 9 o'clock, along with David Toms and Shigeki Maruyama, neither of whom would survive the 36-hole cut. He began differently as well.

Where he had bogeyed the first hole in the opening round, he barely missed birdieing the first when his 15-footer hit the rim of the hole but refused to fall. After a fine drive on the second, he pitched inside 20 feet and holed the putt, his first birdie of the championship.

A fine iron shot to the third left him less than 10 feet from a second birdie, but once again the putt slipped past the hole. Els took his par 3, then moved on to the fourth, the 497-yard par 5 that would surrender 70 birdies and three eagles that day. His drive caught the rough, but he dug it out with his five iron and left himself 35 feet from the hole. After two putts for his birdie, Ernie stood two under par for the round and five over for the 22 holes he had played.

The fifth hole at Sandwich measures 420 yards, but its fairway bends left, and while the bend is far beyond the reach of most golfers, Els hits the ball a very long way. As he stepped onto the tee, he waved for the marshals up ahead to move the gallery back so he could cut the corner. Again with the wind at his back, he moved into the ball with his deceptively liquid swing and ripped it over the knoll where the gallery had stood, pitched to about 15 feet, and once again missed a birdie opening.

He hit another huge drive on the seventh, but again got no reward. Usually outwardly unperturbed, Els claimed later, "That made me hot."

Perhaps, but it changed nothing. He finished the first nine without another birdie, and coming back lost a stroke at the 11th, a 242-yard par 3, where he left his tee shot well short of the green, then won it back on the 13th with a five iron inside 10 feet and, finally, a putt that fell. Two under par once again, Els picked up his final birdie on the 17th, a very difficult par 4 of 428 yards, with a six iron to 12 feet and another putt that fell.

Ernie Els climbed from a tie for 101st to a tie for 16th.

**S K Ho was taking his place alongside
K J Choi and numerous ladies, such as
Se Ri Pak, as prominent Koreans in
world golf.**

With 34 on the home nine, Els had thrust himself back into the championship.

Finding Ho sharing second place probably surprised the gallery at least as much as finding Curtis so close behind. He had been a puzzle. Someone asked Els what he knew of this newcomer to the Open. Els could offer only the obvious.

"He has a shorter surname than me."

True enough, but in the first round Ho had eight strokes fewer than Els, and with his 73 in the second round, he still had three fewer strokes than Ernie and rested in second place alongside Bjorn, the fiery tempered Dane who had cost himself a two-stroke penalty on Thursday with a fit of temper. After failing to recover from a greenside bunker at the 17th, Bjorn slashed at the sand, a violation of the rules, since his ball still lay in that sand. This would cost him heavily later in the week.

By contrast, Ho played pretty much within himself, letting his golf speak loudly.

He comes from Korea, where he is known as Hur Suk-ho. His surname is Hur, but he has the nickname "S K" among friends, and he decided a couple of years ago to call himself S K Ho, an easier name for foreigners to pronounce. His father owns a driving range in Pusan, a city that became prominent in the early days of the Korean War, which began in the summer of 1950 and ended three years later, 50 years before Ho's arrival in Britain.

Since Korea has few professional tournaments, he played his golf in Japan, where he had won the 2002 Juken Sangyo Open in Hiroshima and ranked 17th on

In the Words of the Competitors…

"

"It wasn't easy out there the last couple of days but I have hung in there. I would like to be a little better, but unfortunately I left myself some shots coming in yesterday, and you pay for those."

—Sergio Garcia

"My (right index) finger is (bandaged and) swollen up very badly, after I hit a buried lie on the seventh. I injured it last week at Loch Lomond when I also played from a buried lie."

—John Daly

"I just haven't played to my ability, and I had a few bad breaks. Some bad tee shots ended up in the wrong places."

—Bernhard Langer

"I was not happy with the (5, 5) finish. It feels like I've spoilt two days' work in 15 minutes."

—Andrew Oldcorn

"I'm trying to keep my same focus, my same attitude I've carried for the last month. It seems to be working. This was a great day, a beautiful round of golf for me."

—Kenny Perry

"Anybody who has made the cut right now has a chance to win this golf tournament."

—Greg Norman

"

Vijay Singh fought back with 70 including a birdie 3 on the last hole.

five iron into the 11th that settled 12 feet from the hole. Davis ran it in for the birdie.

Back to two under for the round, Love played a decent approach into the 12th about 30 feet from the hole, but he ran his first putt six feet past and missed coming back. Playing safe from the 13th tee, Love hit a three iron that flew off line to the left and dived into knee-high grass. An alert marshal placed his cap over the spot to mark it, but it still cost Love one more stroke.

Then came the lucky break at the 14th, which saved him one stroke at least. Still, he lost another at the 17th, where his approach settled in a bunker so close to its sheer, revetted face he needed two shots to recover and did well to salvage a bogey 5. In danger of losing yet another stroke on the home hole, where he drove into the right rough, he slashed his next shot across the fairway and into the shallow valley left of the green, popped his third against the rise to the green, and ran it within a foot of the hole, closing his round with a par 4.

"Too many 5s on the second nine," Love said as he finished, "and the wind never let up." Then he commented on the location of the holes on the greens, saying, "Some of the pin placements were the hardest I've ever seen."

At least Love would be around to see more of them the next day, but

Finishing in the early evening, Nick Faldo celebrated his 46th birthday by making the cut on 150.

Craig Parry (far left) returned a second 73 to be tied for 16th place. Marco Ruiz of Paraguay (left) had a share of fourth place in his first Open.

Excerpts from the
Press

Jim Furyk (above), who recently won the US Open, was off after rounds of 74 and 78. Below, Greg Norman's score rose 10 strokes to 79, but he was under the cut.

a number of players of note would not. The 36-hole cut fell at 150, eight over par, and caught such quality players as Jim Furyk, who had won the US Open a month earlier, David Toms, a former USPGA champion, and Jose Maria Olazabal, along with Bernhard Langer and former Open champions Paul Lawrie, Sandy Lyle, who had won the 1985 championship at Sandwich, and David Duval, the 2001 champion. Duval's collapse approaches the tragic. He posted 83-78–161 two years after playing stunning golf at Royal Lytham and St Annes.

Gary Wolstenholme, the Amateur champion, shot 82 in the second round and bid farewell with 156, as did Ricky Barnes, the US Amateur champion, who finished with 153. Justin Rose, who had played so well at Muirfield in 2002, shot 159 this week and was also leaving.

Round Two Hole Summary

HOLE	PAR	EAGLES	BIRDIES	PARS	BOGEYS	D. BOGEYS	HIGHER	RANK	AVERAGE
1	4	0	5	78	53	14	2	1	4.54
2	4	0	16	102	30	4	0	13	4.15
3	3	0	13	99	37	2	1	12	3.20
4	5	3	70	71	8	0	0	18	4.55
5	4	0	18	104	29	1	0	16	4.09
6	3	0	9	99	41	3	0	10	3.25
7	5	5	67	71	8	1	0	17	4.56
8	4	0	9	74	57	11	1	3	4.49
9	4	0	17	67	60	7	1	6	4.40
OUT	**36**	**8**	**224**	**765**	**323**	**43**	**5**		**37.22**
10	4	0	9	79	57	6	1	5	4.42
11	3	0	8	89	53	2	0	9	3.32
12	4	0	18	102	30	2	0	15	4.11
13	4	0	26	82	40	4	0	13	4.15
14	5	0	17	81	34	10	10	4	5.47
15	4	0	7	84	57	4	0	7	4.38
16	3	0	13	96	39	4	0	11	3.22
17	4	0	5	82	52	11	2	2	4.49
18	4	0	6	94	43	8	1	8	4.37
IN	**35**	**0**	**109**	**789**	**405**	**51**	**14**		**37.93**
TOTAL	**71**	**8**	**333**	**1554**	**728**	**94**	**19**		**75.15**

My Favourite
Open

2000 ST ANDREWS

John Lindesay-Bethune
Former R&A Captain

"Any Open at St Andrews is special but this was the Millennium Open and we had the best player as the champion."

False Hopes In Light Winds

By Robert Sommers

Like learning the alphabet, it has been drummed into us so thoroughly we know without question that links golf courses need wind, and lots of it, to hold their own against the game's elite players. True for most, perhaps, but judging from the evidence, Royal St George's stands as the exception.

While it is true that a brisk wind swept across Sandwich during the first round, it had eased considerably over the last two days, and we certainly did not see a frenzied assault on its par of 71. Only nine men shot in the 60s in the second round, and with the field cut to the low 73 scorers for the third, just eight shot in the 60s and 11 more shot 70, one under par.

No one among this group of exceptional golfers could quite get a grip on Royal St George's. Just when they believed they had, the strokes they had won evaporated through unpredictable bounces, putts that broke in two or three directions, and escape-proof bunkers.

Tiger Woods holed out at the seventh for his second eagle 3.

For a time Tiger Woods looked as if he had mastered it when he breezed out in 31, five under par, but instead the course took three of those strokes back on the homeward nine, and Woods shot 69.

Furthermore, after 54 holes, only Thomas Bjorn, Vijay Singh, Kenny Perry, and Fredrik Jacobson had played two rounds under par 71, and of those, Bjorn remained the only man with a three-round score under par— and that by one bare stroke.

After 54 holes, Bjorn led the field with 212. He posted 69, a round that could have been much better. One stroke behind came Davis Love III, who returned a frustrating 72, which left him at level-par 213.

Singh moved from a tie for 11th place into a tie for third with a weird round, first taking strokes away, then giving them back, and reclaiming them once more on his way to 69 as well. He had 214 for the 54 holes, and shared third place with Woods, Perry, Sergio Garcia, who engineered a miracle of his own, and the persistent American Ben Curtis, who shot 70, his best round of the week so far.

Both Pierre Fulke, a stocky 5-foot-8 Swede, and Nick Faldo returned 67s, the best scores of the week, but Ernie Els made up no ground with 72, and Hennie

What A Surprise! Curtis Is Champion

By Robert Sommers

At the mention of the name Ben Curtis, almost everyone at Royal St George's would turn to whomever stood alongside and ask pretty much the same question: Ben who? Even though Curtis had played 13 tournaments this year on the USPGA Tour, hardly anyone at Sandwich knew him, not even other Americans.

But Vijay Singh knew him. Singh had been paired with Curtis two weeks earlier in the last round of the Western Open, the tournament where Curtis earned a place in the Open Championship field. Singh shot 66 that day and placed 11th. Curtis shot 68 and tied for 13th, assuring him an Open spot.

Singh had been impressed. Speaking to his wife, Ardena, Vijay said of Curtis, "This guy can play. He's no pushover. He's got a very good short game, he's a great putter, and he keeps the ball in play."

Ben Curtis made himself known at Royal St George's.

"That's what he did today," Singh said.

It came about that Curtis won the Open Championship while four of the game's best players bumbled their way to second through fourth places.

With the trophy now at his side, Curtis told those crowded in for his interview at the press tent, "Right now many people are probably saying, 'Well, he really doesn't belong there,' but I know I do and that's all that matters."

Over the last four testing holes, only Curtis holed a putt of any length, while Thomas Bjorn played them in four over par, Tiger Woods in two over, and Singh and Davis Love III in one over.

Curtis played them in two over as well, but facing a breaking eight-foot putt to save par on the 18th, Curtis rolled it in. The par 4 saved him; it held his total score at one under par, just enough to beat Bjorn by one stroke. With a round of 69 and a total of 283, only Curtis, the game's 396th ranked player, had beaten Royal St George's formidable par.

Any of four men could have won, but not one could tame those last four difficult holes. Woods could have won, but he overshot the 15th with his approach and dropped one stroke there, then left his second shot

Round Four Hole Summary

HOLE	PAR	EAGLES	BIRDIES	PARS	BOGEYS	D. BOGEYS	HIGHER	RANK	AVERAGE
1	4	0	6	37	27	3	0	4	4.37
2	4	0	14	49	10	0	0	14	3.95
3	3	0	11	43	19	0	0	10	3.11
4	5	0	38	32	3	0	0	17	4.52
5	4	0	11	45	15	2	0	10	4.11
6	3	0	7	57	9	0	0	13	3.03
7	5	5	42	24	2	0	0	18	4.32
8	4	0	5	42	24	2	0	5	4.32
9	4	0	13	46	11	3	0	12	4.06
OUT	36	5	147	375	120	10	0		35.77
10	4	0	8	46	16	2	1	8	4.21
11	3	0	7	41	24	1	0	7	3.26
12	4	0	19	45	8	1	0	16	3.88
13	4	0	8	49	15	1	0	9	4.12
14	5	0	22	38	11	2	0	15	4.90
15	4	0	2	41	27	3	0	3	4.43
16	3	0	8	42	18	5	0	6	3.27
17	4	0	2	30	36	5	0	1	4.60
18	4	0	1	40	31	1	0	2	4.44
IN	35	0	77	372	186	21	1		37.11
TOTAL	71	5	224	747	306	31	1		72.88

Kenny Perry shot 73 and settled for a share of eighth place.

Sergio Garcia (next page) took 74 and dropped to a 10th-place tie.

While a few had played well, others had not. S K Ho, the neophyte Korean, had hung close to the lead through the first three rounds, but posted a 77 and fell into a tie for 28th place, and Phillip Price, tied with Curtis as the day began, shot 73.

Sergio Garcia, two strokes behind Bjorn going into the round, birdied only two holes and bogeyed five, shot 74, and joined Otto in a 10th-place tie.

Norman had been 48 years old at the time of the 2003 Open, two years older than Faldo, and Nick had played better.

Faldo had teed off at 1.20, with Jacobson. His loyal fans cheered when he birdied the fifth, but when he holed a long putt at the seventh for an eagle 3, they erupted in an ear-splitting cheer.

Although Faldo had barely made the cut, he had shot 67 in the third round, and now he stood three

My Favourite
Open

1984 ST ANDREWS

Sir Michael Bonallack
Former R&A Secretary
and Captain

"Seve Ballesteros and Tom
Watson came to those last two
holes close together, and again
we had the two best players in
the game settling the championship. Then Seve birdied the
last about when Tom hit his
approach onto the road at the
17th."

In the Words of
the Competitors…

"

"I'm glad I came. Definitely."
—Ben Curtis

"Too many mistakes on the turn cost me. Coming down the stretch you can't make any bogeys. And I hit a bad shot on 16."
—Vijay Singh

"It wasn't quite enough. If I had putted well, I would have won. If I had hit a few more good shots, I would have won. Thomas, Tiger, and Vijay are all saying the same thing, so it's unfortunate but I gave it my all."
—Davis Love III

"Having not played much, this week I was pleasantly surprised."
—Greg Norman

"I stood on the 15th tee and had one hand on the trophy. I am disappointed, but not too disappointed. I have come a long way in three weeks."
—Thomas Bjorn

"I had a chance. I was right where I needed to be and just didn't quite make the putts and hit the proper shots. I hit some good shots on the back nine, they just didn't turn out where I wanted to put them."
—Tiger Woods

"

Round of the Day

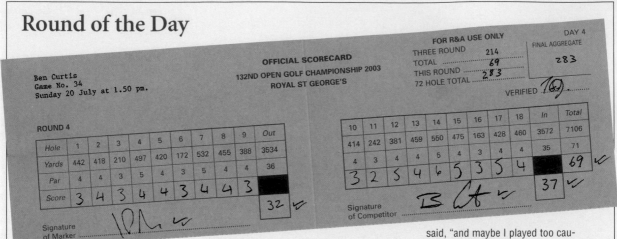

Ben Curtis
Game No. 34
Sunday 20 July at 1.50 pm.

OFFICIAL SCORECARD
132ND OPEN GOLF CHAMPIONSHIP 2003
ROYAL ST GEORGE'S

FOR R&A USE ONLY

THREE ROUND	214
TOTAL	69
THIS ROUND	283
72 HOLE TOTAL	

DAY 4 FINAL AGGREGATE

283

VERIFIED

ROUND 4

Hole	1	2	3	4	5	6	7	8	9	Out
Yards	442	418	210	497	420	172	532	455	388	3534
Par	4	4	3	5	4	3	5	4	4	36
Score	3	4	3	4	4	3	4	4	3	32

Signature of Marker

Hole	10	11	12	13	14	15	16	17	18	In	Total
Yards	414	242	381	459	550	475	163	428	460	3572	7106
Par	4	3	4	4	5	4	3	4	4	35	71
Score	3	2	5	4	6	5	3	5	4	37	69

Signature of Competitor

A round of 69, two under par, and a 283 aggregate were enough for Ben Curtis to become the Open champion. He had four birdies for 32 to the turn and six birdies through the 11th, commanding a two-stroke lead at four under par for the championship. He hit a wedge shot to six feet on the first hole, had two-putt birdies on the two par-5 holes, the fourth and the seventh, and one putt on the ninth. Starting the second nine, he holed from 20 feet on the 10th and from 15 feet on the 11th.

He finished with four bogeys on the 12th, 14th, 15th, and 17th holes, and said he was "shaking in my boots" as he came in with 37. "I was playing hard coming in," Curtis said, "and maybe I played too cautiously, instead of playing as I had been. I hit a couple of bad shots and it cost me. It put a lot of pressure on my short game."

The last putt on the 18th was for par 4 from eight feet. "I didn't know how important it was," Curtis said. "I didn't know about Bjorn on 16, but I knew I had to make it to give myself a chance."

Low Scores

Low First Nine

Peter Fowler	32
Ben Curtis	32

Low Second Nine

Davis Love III	33
Mark McNulty	33
Fredrik Jacobson	33

Low Round

Stewart Cink	68
Greg Norman	68
Brian Davis	68

Curtis went out in 32, then birdied the 10th and 11th, building a two-stroke lead.

rough and flew a seven iron onto the front of the green. His first putt just missed falling for an eagle 3, but he took the birdie and dropped to three under par for the round, two under for the championship.

After a routine par on the eighth, Curtis ran off three straight birdies that put him in command of the Open. He could have birdied four, but his putt on the eighth stopped inches short of falling. Left with an awkward lie in the short rough at the ninth, he handled it beautifully, pitched inside two feet, and dipped four under par.

Out in 32, Curtis pitched to 20 feet and birdied the 10th, then rifled a five iron to 15 feet and birdied the 11th. He had played those 11 holes in six under par, stood five under for the championship, six under for the round, and led the field by two strokes. Still, seven tough holes lay ahead.

Meantime, Bjorn, Love, Singh, and Woods trailed behind him, and they weren't finished.

Love could do nothing right, played shabby golf throughout the first nine, shot 39, three over par, and although he settled himself on the homeward nine, his closing 72 wasn't nearly enough. Perry began with a three-putt green and never made a move, and Garcia showed little spark and had no effect on the outcome.

All the while Woods remained the most dangerous player in the field simply because he might shoot anything at all. He barely missed holing a 30-footer on the first hole, played a nice running shot into the second and came away with another par, one-putted the third for still another, and then birdied three of the next four holes, dipping to two under par for the championship.

His birdie on the fourth showed just what he might do. Bunkered after his second shot, Woods pitched out to 10 feet and holed for the 4, then barely missed an eagle on the seventh.

At that time Singh had passed both Bjorn and Curtis and taken over first place at three under par, followed by Woods at two under, Curtis, two under through the eighth, and Bjorn, two under through six.

Phillip Price played alongside the champion.

Davis Love III (left) and Thomas Bjorn were in the final game.

In the Words of the Competitors…

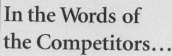

"I'm glad I came. Definitely."

—Ben Curtis

"Too many mistakes on the turn cost me. Coming down the stretch you can't make any bogeys. And I hit a bad shot on 16."

—Vijay Singh

"It wasn't quite enough. If I had putted well, I would have won. If I had hit a few more good shots, I would have won. Thomas, Tiger, and Vijay are all saying the same thing, so it's unfortunate but I gave it my all."

—Davis Love III

"Having not played much, this week I was pleasantly surprised."

—Greg Norman

"I stood on the 15th tee and had one hand on the trophy. I am disappointed, but not too disappointed. I have come a long way in three weeks."

—Thomas Bjorn

"I had a chance. I was right where I needed to be and just didn't quite make the putts and hit the proper shots. I hit some good shots on the back nine, they just didn't turn out where I wanted to put them."

—Tiger Woods

The Open Championship

Results

Year	Champion	Score	Margin	Runners-up	Venue
1860	Willie Park Snr	174	2	Tom Morris Snr	Prestwick
1861	Tom Morris Snr	163	4	Willie Park Snr	Prestwick
1862	Tom Morris Snr	163	13	Willie Park Snr	Prestwick
1863	Willie Park Snr	168	2	Tom Morris Snr	Prestwick
1864	Tom Morris Snr	167	2	Andrew Strath	Prestwick
1865	Andrew Strath	162	2	Willie Park Snr	Prestwick
1866	Willie Park Snr	169	2	David Park	Prestwick
1867	Tom Morris Snr	170	2	Willie Park Snr	Prestwick
1868	Tom Morris Jnr	154	3	Tom Morris Snr	Prestwick
1869	Tom Morris Jnr	157	11	Bob Kirk	Prestwick
1870	Tom Morris Jnr	149	12	Bob Kirk, David Strath	Prestwick
1871	*No Competition*				
1872	Tom Morris Jnr	166	3	David Strath	Prestwick
1873	Tom Kidd	179	1	Jamie Anderson	St Andrews
1874	Mungo Park	159	2	Tom Morris Jnr	Musselburgh
1875	Willie Park Snr	166	2	Bob Martin	Prestwick
1876	Bob Martin	176	—	David Strath	St Andrews
	(Martin was awarded the title when Strath refused to play-off)				
1877	Jamie Anderson	160	2	Bob Pringle	Musselburgh
1878	Jamie Anderson	157	2	Bob Kirk	Prestwick
1879	Jamie Anderson	169	3	James Allan, Andrew Kirkaldy	St Andrews
1880	Bob Ferguson	162	5	Peter Paxton	Musselburgh
1881	Bob Ferguson	170	3	Jamie Anderson	Prestwick
1882	Bob Ferguson	171	3	Willie Fernie	St Andrews
1883	Willie Fernie	158	Playoff	Bob Ferguson	Musselburgh
1884	Jack Simpson	160	4	Douglas Rolland, Willie Fernie	Prestwick
1885	Bob Martin	171	1	Archie Simpson	St Andrews
1886	David Brown	157	2	Willie Campbell	Musselburgh
1887	Willie Park Jnr	161	1	Bob Martin	Prestwick
1888	Jack Burns	171	1	David Anderson Jnr, Ben Sayers	St Andrews
1889	Willie Park Jnr	155	Playoff	Andrew Kirkaldy	Musselburgh
1890	*John Ball Jnr	164	3	Willie Fernie, Archie Simpson	Prestwick
1891	Hugh Kirkaldy	166	2	Willie Fernie, Andrew Kirkaldy	St Andrews
(From 1892 the competition was extended to 72 holes)					
1892	*Harold Hilton	305	3	*John Ball Jnr, Hugh Kirkaldy, Sandy Herd	Muirfield

Sandy Lyle (1985)

Paul Lawrie (1999)

Year	Champion	Score	Margin	Runners-up	Venue
1893	Willie Auchterlonie	322	2	*John Laidlay	Prestwick
1894	J.H. Taylor	326	5	Douglas Rolland	Sandwich
1895	J.H. Taylor	322	4	Sandy Herd	St Andrews
1896	Harry Vardon	316	Playoff	J.H. Taylor	Muirfield
1897	*Harold Hilton	314	1	James Braid	Hoylake
1898	Harry Vardon	307	1	Willie Park Jnr	Prestwick
1899	Harry Vardon	310	5	Jack White	Sandwich
1900	J.H. Taylor	309	8	Harry Vardon	St Andrews
1901	James Braid	309	3	Harry Vardon	Muirfield
1902	Sandy Herd	307	1	Harry Vardon, James Braid	Hoylake
1903	Harry Vardon	300	6	Tom Vardon	Prestwick
1904	Jack White	296	1	James Braid, J.H. Taylor	Sandwich
1905	James Braid	318	5	J.H. Taylor, Rowland Jones	St Andrews
1906	James Braid	300	4	J.H. Taylor	Muirfield
1907	Arnaud Massy	312	2	J.H. Taylor	Hoylake
1908	James Braid	291	8	Tom Ball	Prestwick
1909	J.H. Taylor	295	6	James Braid, Tom Ball	Deal
1910	James Braid	299	4	Sandy Herd	St Andrews
1911	Harry Vardon	303	Playoff	Arnaud Massy	Sandwich
1912	Ted Ray	295	4	Harry Vardon	Muirfield
1913	J.H. Taylor	304	8	Ted Ray	Hoylake
1914	Harry Vardon	306	3	J.H. Taylor	Prestwick
1915-1919 No Championship					
1920	George Duncan	303	2	Sandy Herd	Deal
1921	Jock Hutchison	296	Playoff	*Roger Wethered	St Andrews
1922	Walter Hagen	300	1	George Duncan, Jim Barnes	Sandwich
1923	Arthur Havers	295	1	Walter Hagen	Troon
1924	Walter Hagen	301	1	Ernest Whitcombe	Hoylake
1925	Jim Barnes	300	1	Archie Compston, Ted Ray	Prestwick
1926	*Robert T. Jones Jnr	291	2	Al Watrous	Royal Lytham
1927	*Robert T. Jones Jnr	285	6	Aubrey Boomer, Fred Robson	St Andrews
1928	Walter Hagen	292	2	Gene Sarazen	Sandwich
1929	Walter Hagen	292	6	John Farrell	Muirfield
1930	*Robert T. Jones Jnr	291	2	Leo Diegel, Macdonald Smith	Hoylake

The Open Championship

Records

MOST VICTORIES
6, Harry Vardon, 1896-98-99-1903-11-14
5, James Braid, 1901-05-06-08-10; J.H. Taylor, 1894-95-1900-09-13; Peter Thomson, 1954-55-56-58-65; Tom Watson, 1975-77-80-82-83

MOST TIMES RUNNER-UP OR JOINT RUNNER-UP
7, Jack Nicklaus, 1964-67-68-72-76-77-79
6, J.H. Taylor, 1896-1904-05-06-07-14

OLDEST WINNER
Old Tom Morris, 46 years 99 days, 1867
Harry Vardon, 44 years 41 days, 1914
Roberto de Vicenzo, 44 years 93 days, 1967

YOUNGEST WINNER
Young Tom Morris, 17 years 5 months 8 days, 1868
Willie Auchterlonie, 21 years 24 days, 1893
Severiano Ballesteros, 22 years 3 months 12 days, 1979

YOUNGEST AND OLDEST COMPETITOR
Young Tom Morris, 14 years 4 months 4 days, 1865
Gene Sarazen, 74 years 5 months 8 days, 1976

BIGGEST MARGIN OF VICTORY
13 strokes, Old Tom Morris, 1862
12 strokes, Young Tom Morris, 1870
11 strokes, Young Tom Morris, 1869
8 strokes, J.H. Taylor, 1900 and 1913; James Braid, 1908; Tiger Woods, 2000

LOWEST WINNING AGGREGATES
267 (66, 68, 69, 64), Greg Norman, Royal St George's, 1993
268 (68, 70, 65, 65), Tom Watson, Turnberry, 1977; (69, 66, 67, 66), Nick Price, Turnberry, 1994
269 (67, 66, 67, 69), Tiger Woods, St Andrews, 2000

Tiger Woods (2000)

LOWEST AGGREGATE IN RELATION TO PAR
269 (19 under par), Tiger Woods, St Andrews, 2000
270 (18 under par), Nick Faldo, St Andrews, 1990

LOWEST AGGREGATES BY RUNNER-UP
269 (68, 70, 65, 66), Jack Nicklaus, Turnberry, 1977; (69, 63, 70, 67), Nick Faldo, Royal St George's, 1993; (68, 66, 68, 67), Jesper Parnevik, Turnberry, 1994

LOWEST AGGREGATES BY AN AMATEUR
281 (68, 72, 70, 71), Iain Pyman, Royal St George's, 1993; (75, 66, 70, 70), Tiger Woods, Royal Lytham, 1996

LOWEST INDIVIDUAL ROUND
63, Mark Hayes, second round, Turnberry, 1977; Isao Aoki, third round, Muirfield, 1980; Greg Norman, second round, Turnberry, 1986; Paul Broadhurst, third round, St Andrews, 1990; Jodie Mudd, fourth round, Royal Birkdale, 1991; Nick Faldo, second round, and Payne Stewart, fourth round, Royal St George's, 1993

LOWEST INDIVIDUAL ROUND BY AN AMATEUR
66, Frank Stranahan, fourth round, Troon, 1950; Tiger Woods, second round, Royal Lytham, 1996; Justin Rose, second round, Royal Birkdale, 1998

LOWEST FIRST ROUND
64, Craig Stadler, Royal Birkdale, 1983; Christy O'Connor Jnr., Royal St George's, 1985; Rodger Davis, Muirfield, 1987; Raymond Floyd and Steve Pate, Muirfield, 1992

LOWEST SECOND ROUND
63, Mark Hayes, Turnberry, 1977; Greg Norman, Turnberry, 1986; Nick Faldo, Royal St George's, 1993

Mark Calcavecchia (1989)

LOWEST THIRD ROUND
63, Isao Aoki, Muirfield, 1980; Paul Broadhurst, St Andrews, 1990

LOWEST FOURTH ROUND
63, Jodie Mudd, Royal Birkdale, 1991; Payne Stewart, Royal St George's, 1993

LOWEST FIRST 36 HOLES
130 (66, 64), Nick Faldo, Muirfield, 1992

LOWEST SECOND 36 HOLES
130 (65, 65), Tom Watson, Turnberry, 1977; (64, 66), Ian Baker-Finch, Royal Birkdale, 1991; (66, 64), Anders Forsbrand, Turnberry, 1994

LOWEST MIDDLE 36 HOLES
130 (66, 64), Fuzzy Zoeller, Turnberry, 1994

LOWEST FIRST 54 HOLES
198 (67, 67, 64), Tom Lehman, Royal Lytham, 1996
199 (67, 65, 67), Nick Faldo, St Andrews, 1990; (66, 64, 69), Nick Faldo, Muirfield, 1992

LOWEST FINAL 54 HOLES
199 (66, 67, 66), Nick Price, Turnberry, 1994

LOWEST 9 HOLES
28, Denis Durnian, first 9, Royal Birkdale, 1983
29, Peter Thomson and Tom Haliburton, first 9, Royal Lytham, 1958; Tony Jacklin, first 9, St Andrews, 1970; Bill Longmuir, first 9, Royal Lytham, 1979; David J. Russell, first 9, Royal Lytham, 1988; Ian Baker-Finch and Paul Broadhurst, first 9, St Andrews, 1990; Ian Baker-Finch, first 9, Royal Birkdale, 1991; Paul McGinley, first 9, Royal Lytham, 1996; Ernie Els, first 9, Muirfield, 2002

SUCCESSIVE VICTORIES
4, Young Tom Morris, 1868-72 (no championship in 1871).
3, Jamie Anderson, 1877-79; Bob Ferguson, 1880-82, Peter Thomson, 1954-56
2, Old Tom Morris, 1861-62; J.H. Taylor, 1894-95; Harry Vardon, 1898-99; James Braid, 1905-06; Bobby Jones, 1926-27; Walter Hagen, 1928-29; Bobby Locke, 1949-50; Arnold Palmer, 1961-62; Lee Trevino, 1971-72; Tom Watson, 1982-83

VICTORIES BY AMATEURS
3, Bobby Jones, 1926-27-30
2, Harold Hilton, 1892-97
1, John Ball, 1890
Roger Wethered lost a playoff in 1921

CHAMPIONS IN FIRST APPEARANCE
Willie Park, Prestwick, 1860; Tom Kidd, St Andrews, 1873; Mungo Park, Musselburgh, 1874; Harold Hilton, Muirfield, 1892; Jock Hutchison, St Andrews, 1921; Densmore Shute, St Andrews, 1933; Ben Hogan, Carnoustie, 1953; Tony Lema, St Andrews, 1964; Tom Watson, Carnoustie, 1975; Ben Curtis, Sandwich, 2003

BIGGEST SPAN BETWEEN FIRST AND LAST VICTORIES
19 years, J.H. Taylor, 1894-1913
18 years, Harry Vardon, 1896-1914
15 years, Gary Player, 1959-74
14 years, Henry Cotton, 1934-48

BIGGEST SPAN BETWEEN VICTORIES
11 years, Henry Cotton, 1937-48

CHAMPIONS IN THREE DECADES
Harry Vardon, 1896, 1903, 1911
J.H. Taylor, 1894, 1900, 1913
Gary Player, 1959, 1968, 1974

Nick Faldo (1987, 1990, 1992)

HIGHEST NUMBER OF TOP-FIVE FINISHES
16, J.H. Taylor, Jack Nicklaus
15, Harry Vardon, James Braid

HIGHEST NUMBER OF ROUNDS UNDER PAR
61, Jack Nicklaus
49, Nick Faldo
40, Tom Watson

HIGHEST NUMBER OF AGGREGATES UNDER PAR
14, Jack Nicklaus
13, Nick Faldo

MOST CONSECUTIVE ROUNDS UNDER 70
7, Ernie Els, 1993-94

OUTRIGHT LEADER AFTER EVERY ROUND
Ted Ray, 1912; Bobby Jones, 1927; Gene Sarazen, 1932; Henry Cotton, 1934; Tom Weiskopf, 1973

LEADER AFTER EVERY ROUND INCLUDING TIES
Harry Vardon, 1899 and 1903; J.H. Taylor, 1900; Lee Trevino, 1971; Gary Player, 1974

RECORD LEADS (SINCE 1892)
After 18 holes:
4 strokes, James Braid, 1908; Bobby Jones, 1927; Henry Cotton, 1934; Christy O'Connor Jnr., 1985
After 36 holes:
9 strokes, Henry Cotton, 1934
After 54 holes:
10 strokes, Henry Cotton, 1934
7 strokes, Tony Lema, 1964

BIGGEST LEADS BY NON-CHAMPIONS
After 54 holes:
5 strokes, Macdonald Smith, 1925; Jean Van de Velde, 1999

CHAMPIONS WITH EACH ROUND LOWER THAN PREVIOUS ONE
Jack White, 1904, Sandwich, (80, 75, 72, 69)
James Braid, 1906, Muirfield, (77, 76, 74, 73)
Henry Cotton, 1937, Carnoustie, (74, 73, 72, 71)
Ben Hogan, 1953, Carnoustie, (73, 71, 70, 68)
Gary Player, 1959, Muirfield, (75, 71, 70, 68)

CHAMPION WITH FOUR ROUNDS THE SAME
Densmore Shute, 1933, St Andrews, (73, 73, 73, 73) (excluding the playoff)

BIGGEST VARIATION BETWEEN ROUNDS OF A CHAMPION
14 strokes, Henry Cotton, 1934, second round 65, fourth round 79
11 strokes, Jack White, 1904, first round 80, fourth round 69; Greg Norman, 1986, first round 74, second round 63, third round 74

BIGGEST VARIATION BETWEEN TWO ROUNDS
20 strokes, R.G. French, 1938, second round 71, third round 91; Colin Montgomerie, 2002, second round 64, third round 84
19 strokes, R.H. Pemberton, 1938, second round 72, third round 91
18 strokes, A. Tingey Jnr., 1923, first round 94, second round 76
17 strokes, Jack Nicklaus, 1981, first round 83, second round 66; Ian Baker-Finch, 1986, first round 86, second round 69

BEST COMEBACK BY CHAMPIONS
After 18 holes:
Harry Vardon, 1896, 11 strokes behind the leader
After 36 holes:
George Duncan, 1920, 13 strokes behind the leader
After 54 holes:
Paul Lawrie, 1999, 10 strokes behind the leader

CHAMPIONS WITH FOUR ROUNDS UNDER 70
Greg Norman, 1993, Royal St George's, (66, 68, 69, 64); Nick Price, 1994, Turnberry, (69, 66, 67, 66); Tiger Woods, 2000, St Andrews, (67, 66, 67, 69)
Of non-champions:
Ernie Els, 1993, Royal St George's, (68, 69, 69, 68); Jesper Parnevik, 1994, Turnberry, (68, 66, 68, 67)

BEST FINISHING ROUND BY A CHAMPION
64, Greg Norman, Royal St George's, 1993
65, Tom Watson, Turnberry, 1977; Severiano Ballesteros, Royal Lytham, 1988; Justin Leonard, Royal Troon, 1997

WORST ROUND BY A CHAMPION SINCE 1939
78, Fred Daly, third round, Hoylake, 1947
76, Paul Lawrie, third round, Carnoustie, 1999

Nick Price (1994)

WORST FINISHING ROUND BY A CHAMPION SINCE 1939
75, Sam Snead, St Andrews, 1946

BEST OPENING ROUND BY A CHAMPION
66, Peter Thomson, Royal Lytham, 1958; Nick Faldo, Muirfield, 1992; Greg Norman, Royal St George's, 1993

BIGGEST RECOVERY IN 18 HOLES BY A CHAMPION
George Duncan, Deal, 1920, was 13 strokes behind the leader, Abe Mitchell, after 36 holes and level after 54

MOST APPEARANCES
46, Gary Player
37, Jack Nicklaus

MOST APPEARANCES ON FINAL DAY (SINCE 1892)
32, Jack Nicklaus
31, Alex Herd
30, J.H. Taylor
27, Harry Vardon, James Braid
26, Peter Thomson, Gary Player
23, Dai Rees
22, Henry Cotton

MOST APPEARANCES BEFORE FIRST VICTORY
16, Nick Price, 1994
14, Mark O'Meara, 1998

MOST APPEARANCES WITHOUT A VICTORY
29, Dai Rees
28, Sam Torrance
27, Neil Coles

CHAMPIONSHIP WITH HIGHEST NUMBER OF ROUNDS UNDER 70
148, Turnberry, 1994

CHAMPIONSHIP SINCE 1946 WITH THE FEWEST ROUNDS UNDER 70
St Andrews, 1946; Hoylake, 1947; Portrush, 1951; Hoylake, 1956; Carnoustie, 1968. All had only two rounds under 70.

LONGEST COURSE
Carnoustie, 1999, 7361 yards

COURSES MOST OFTEN USED
St Andrews, 26; Prestwick, 24; Muirfield, 15; Sandwich, 13; Hoylake and Royal Lytham, 10; Royal Birkdale, 8; Royal Troon, 7; Musselburgh and Carnoustie, 6; Turnberry, 3; Deal, 2; Royal Portrush and Prince's, 1

Ernie Els (2002)

Tom Watson (1975, 1977, 1980, 1982, 1983)

HOLE			1	2	3	4	5	6	7	8	9	10	11	12	13	14	15	16	17	18	
PAR	POSITION		4	4	3	5	4	3	5	4	4	4	3	4	4	5	4	3	4	4	TOTAL
S K Ho	T4	Round 1	5	4	4	4	4	3	4	5	3	4	3	3	4	6	3	3	4	4	70
Korea	T2	Round 2	4	4	2	3	4	3	5	5	5	4	4	4	5	5	3	4	5		73
£26,000	T8	Round 3	5	4	3	4	4	2	5	4	5	4	3	4	5	5	3	4	4		72
	T28	Round 4	6	3	4	5	5	3	5	4	4	4	4	4	5	5	4	3	5	4	77 -292
Stewart Cink	T54	Round 1	4	6	3	5	5	3	5	5	4	3	3	4	4	6	3	3	4	5	75
USA	T59	Round 2	5	5	2	4	4	3	5	5	8	5	2	4	3	5	4	3	4	4	75
£18,778	T66	Round 3	4	5	3	5	4	3	3	4	4	4	3	3	4	8	6	3	4	5	75
	T34	Round 4	4	4	3	4	4	3	3	5	4	4	2	4	5	4	4	3	4	4	68 -293
Bob Estes	T82	Round 1	4	4	3	6	4	4	4	6	5	4	3	5	5	5	4	3	4	4	77
USA	T35	Round 2	4	4	2	5	5	3	4	4	5	4	2	3	3	5	5	4	4	5	71
£18,778	T61	Round 3	4	4	4	5	4	3	4	5	5	4	4	4	4	6	6	2	4	4	76
	T34	Round 4	5	5	2	4	4	2	4	4	3	4	3	4	4	4	5	4	4	4	69 -293
Adam Mednick	T65	Round 1	5	4	4	4	4	3	4	5	4	4	3	4	4	6	5	3	5	5	76
Sweden	T35	Round 2	4	3	3	5	4	4	3	4	4	4	4	4	5	5	5	3	4	4	72
£18,778	T61	Round 3	4	5	3	5	4	3	5	5	4	4	4	4	4	6	4	3	5	4	76
	T34	Round 4	4	4	4	4	3	3	4	4	3	3	4	4	4	4	4	3	5	5	69 -293
Shingo Katayama	T65	Round 1	4	3	3	4	5	4	4	5	6	5	3	4	5	5	4	3	4	5	76
Japan	T48	Round 2	5	3	3	4	4	3	5	5	5	6	4	5	3	4	4	3	4	4	73
£18,778	T49	Round 3	4	4	3	4	5	3	5	4	5	4	3	4	4	5	3	5	4		73
	T34	Round 4	4	4	3	5	4	3	4	3	3	4	4	4	4	5	5	3	5	4	71 -293
Gary Murphy	T19	Round 1	4	3	4	5	4	3	4	4	5	5	3	4	5	5	4	2	4	5	73
Ireland	T28	Round 2	4	4	3	4	3	3	5	4	5	4	3	4	4	7	5	4	4	4	74
£18,778	T34	Round 3	4	4	4	5	4	3	4	5	4	5	4	4	5	6	3	2	4	4	73
	T34	Round 4	4	4	3	5	4	3	4	3	4	5	3	4	5	5	5	4	5	4	73 -293
Duffy Waldorf	T65	Round 1	6	5	3	5	5	3	4	4	4	4	3	5	5	5	4	3	4	4	76
USA	T48	Round 2	4	4	3	4	4	4	5	4	5	4	3	4	3	5	4	3	5	5	73
£18,778	T34	Round 3	4	4	3	4	5	3	4	4	5	5	3	4	4	4	3	3	4	5	71
	T34	Round 4	5	4	3	5	4	3	4	5	3	4	3	4	5	5	4	3	4	5	73 -293
Marco Ruiz	T19	Round 1	6	4	3	4	4	3	5	4	4	4	4	3	4	5	5	3	4	4	73
Paraguay	T4	Round 2	5	4	3	5	4	3	5	4	4	3	2	4	4	4	5	3	4	5	71
£18,778	T27	Round 3	4	5	3	5	4	4	5	5	4	4	4	4	4	5	3	2	4	6	75
	T34	Round 4	4	4	2	4	4	3	5	4	3	4	4	4	5	7	5	3	5	4	74 -293
Jose Coceres	T82	Round 1	4	4	3	4	4	4	5	5	4	3	4	5	4	5	5	3	5	6	77
Argentina	T28	Round 2	5	3	3	4	5	3	4	4	3	5	3	4	3	5	5	3	4	4	70
£18,778	T27	Round 3	4	4	3	4	4	4	4	4	4	3	3	4	5	5	4	3	5	5	72
	T34	Round 4	3	4	3	4	5	3	4	5	5	4	3	5	4	5	5	3	5	4	74 -293
Scott McCarron	T6	Round 1	4	4	3	5	4	3	6	4	4	5	2	3	5	5	4	3	3	4	71
USA	T11	Round 2	5	5	2	4	3	3	4	4	3	4	3	5	4	6	4	4	7	4	74
£18,778	T18	Round 3	5	4	3	4	3	4	4	5	4	4	4	4	4	5	3	5	4		73
	T34	Round 4	5	4	3	4	4	3	5	5	4	4	3	4	3	6	5	4	5	4	75 -293
Rich Beem	T65	Round 1	3	4	3	4	4	4	4	5	4	4	3	5	5	6	5	3	5	5	76
USA	T59	Round 2	5	4	3	4	4	2	6	4	6	3	3	4	4	5	4	4	4	5	74
£14,250	T66	Round 3	4	3	3	5	4	3	5	4	6	4	3	4	4	5	4	4	4	5	75
	T43	Round 4	5	4	3	4	4	3	4	4	4	4	3	3	4	4	4	2	5	5	69 -294
Robert Allenby	T19	Round 1	4	4	4	4	4	4	4	5	3	5	3	4	4	5	4	3	5	4	73
Australia	T35	Round 2	6	5	3	5	4	3	4	4	3	4	3	5	4	5	4	3	6	4	75
£14,250	T49	Round 3	4	4	4	4	4	3	4	5	4	4	4	4	5	5	4	3	5	4	74
	T43	Round 4	5	4	2	5	6	3	4	4	4	4	3	3	4	5	4	4	4	4	72 -294

HOLE			1	2	3	4	5	6	7	8	9	10	11	12	13	14	15	16	17	18	
PAR	POSITION		4	4	3	5	4	3	5	4	4	4	3	4	4	5	4	3	4	4	TOTAL
Tom Byrum	T82	Round 1	5	4	2	6	4	4	5	5	3	5	4	5	3	5	6	2	5	3	77
USA	T48	Round 2	4	4	2	4	4	3	4	3	5	4	4	4	4	6	5	4	5	3	72
£14,250	T34	Round 3	4	5	3	5	4	4	3	4	2	3	4	5	3	5	4	3	5	5	71
	T43	Round 4	4	4	3	5	4	3	5	5	4	4	3	4	3	5	5	2	6	5	74 -294
Tom Lehman	T82	Round 1	5	4	3	5	3	4	5	5	4	4	3	4	3	6	7	3	4	5	77
USA	T59	Round 2	3	4	4	5	5	3	3	5	3	4	3	5	4	6	4	3	5	4	73
£11,864	T49	Round 3	3	5	3	4	3	4	5	4	4	4	4	3	4	5	5	3	4	5	72
	T46	Round 4	4	4	3	5	4	3	4	4	4	4	3	4	4	5	5	4	5	4	73 -295
Markus Brier	T65	Round 1	5	5	3	4	4	4	4	5	6	5	3	4	4	4	4	3	4	5	76
Austria	T28	Round 2	3	3	3	5	4	3	6	4	4	5	3	4	4	5	4	3	4	4	71
£11,864	T44	Round 3	4	5	3	5	4	3	4	5	4	4	4	3	3	5	5	4	5	4	74
	T46	Round 4	4	4	3	5	4	2	4	4	4	4	3	4	4	6	6	3	5	5	74 -295
Anthony Wall	T54	Round 1	5	4	3	5	4	3	5	3	4	4	3	6	5	5	4	4	4	4	75
England	T48	Round 2	5	4	3	4	4	4	4	4	5	4	3	4	5	4	4	4	5	4	74
£11,864	T34	Round 3	5	5	3	4	4	3	4	4	4	4	3	4	3	5	4	3	4	5	71
	T46	Round 4	4	4	4	4	5	4	5	4	5	5	2	4	4	4	4	4	4	5	75 -295
Brad Faxon	T82	Round 1	4	4	3	5	4	3	5	5	4	4	3	5	4	6	4	4	5	5	77
USA	T59	Round 2	4	4	4	4	4	3	4	5	5	4	3	4	5	5	5	2	4	4	73
£11,864	T34	Round 3	4	4	3	4	4	3	5	4	3	5	4	4	4	5	4	3	3	4	70
	T46	Round 4	4	5	2	5	5	3	5	4	4	4	4	4	4	5	5	3	4	5	75 -295
Ian Poulter	T101	Round 1	6	4	3	4	4	3	5	5	4	4	3	3	5	6	4	4	5	6	78
England	T59	Round 2	5	3	3	5	4	3	4	4	4	5	3	4	3	5	4	4	5	4	72
£11,864	T34	Round 3	4	4	3	5	3	3	5	4	4	4	4	3	4	5	4	3	4	4	70
	T46	Round 4	4	3	3	6	5	3	5	6	4	4	3	5	4	5	4	2	4	5	75 -295
Mathew Goggin	T65	Round 1	4	4	3	4	4	4	4	5	5	4	3	3	5	6	4	4	5	5	76
Australia	T35	Round 2	5	4	4	4	3	3	4	4	4	5	3	4	4	5	6	2	4	4	72
£11,864	T18	Round 3	3	4	3	5	4	2	4	5	4	4	4	6	4	4	4	3	3	4	70
	T46	Round 4	5	5	3	4	5	4	4	5	4	5	4	4	3	5	4	5	4	4	77 -295
Fred Couples	T6	Round 1	4	3	3	4	5	2	5	4	4	4	3	4	5	5	4	3	5	4	71
USA	T16	Round 2	4	4	2	5	5	4	4	5	4	5	3	4	4	5	4	4	4	5	75
£11,864	T14	Round 3	4	5	3	4	5	4	5	5	3	4	3	4	4	3	4	2	4	5	71
	T46	Round 4	4	4	4	5	3	4	5	5	3	5	4	3	4	5	6	4	5	5	78 -295
Mark McNulty	T115	Round 1	4	3	3	6	4	4	5	5	4	5	4	4	4	6	5	3	4	6	79
Zimbabwe	T59	Round 2	4	4	3	4	4	3	4	5	3	4	3	4	5	5	4	3	5	4	71
£10,200	T70	Round 3	5	4	4	5	4	3	4	6	5	4	3	4	5	5	5	3	4	4	77
	T53	Round 4	4	4	3	5	5	3	4	4	4	3	3	4	4	4	4	3	4	4	69 -296
Rory Sabbatini	T115	Round 1	4	6	3	5	4	4	4	4	4	4	4	5	4	6	4	4	4	6	79
South Africa	T59	Round 2	4	4	4	4	4	3	5	5	4	4	3	4	5	4	3	3	3	5	71
£10,200	T66	Round 3	4	4	3	6	3	3	5	5	5	4	4	4	4	5	3	5	4		75
	T53	Round 4	5	4	3	4	5	3	4	4	3	4	3	3	4	4	5	3	5	5	71 -296
Michael Campbell	T101	Round 1	4	4	3	3	3	4	6	6	4	5	4	4	5	5	4	4	6	4	78
New Zealand	T59	Round 2	4	5	3	4	3	3	4	4	4	4	4	3	4	6	5	4	4	4	72
£10,200	T61	Round 3	4	4	4	6	4	4	4	5	3	4	3	3	4	5	5	3	4	5	74
	T53	Round 4	4	4	2	4	4	3	5	4	4	5	4	3	5	4	4	4	5	4	72 -296
Trevor Immelman	T82	Round 1	4	4	3	5	3	4	4	4	6	6	3	4	5	6	4	2	5	5	77
South Africa	T59	Round 2	4	4	3	4	3	3	4	4	6	5	3	6	4	5	3	3	5	4	73
£10,200	T49	Round 3	6	4	2	4	4	3	4	5	5	4	3	4	5	5	4	3	4	3	72
	T53	Round 4	4	4	3	4	5	3	6	4	4	5	3	3	4	5	4	4	4	5	74 -296

THE ROYAL
ST. GEORGE'S
GOLF CLUB
SANDWICH

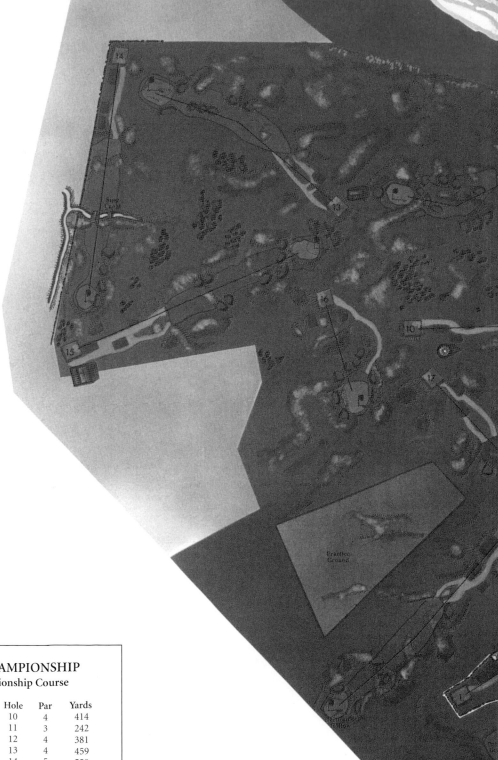

132ND OPEN CHAMPIONSHIP
Card of the Championship Course

Hole	Par	Yards	Hole	Par	Yards
1	4	442	10	4	414
2	4	418	11	3	242
3	3	210	12	4	381
4	5	497	13	4	459
5	4	420	14	5	550
6	3	172	15	4	475
7	5	532	16	3	163
8	4	455	17	4	428
9	4	388	18	4	460
Out	36	3,534	In	35	3,572
			Total	71	7,106